KAUAI'S
GEOLOGIC HISTORY

A SIMPLIFIED GUIDE

UPDATED ED.

Chuck Blay
Robert Siemers

Contents

PREFACE

Since the publication of the first edition of *Kauai's Geologic History* in 1998 we have persistently expanded our knowledge about the natural history of the islands of Hawaii. Our information has grown by continuing to carry out independent research, by preparing for and conducting seminars on geology and ecology for science educators and school groups and by leading numerous nature hikes for island visitors. We are fortunate to live in one of Earth's most magnificent places while performing all of these rewarding activities. It certainly helped us realize even more the two essential elements of the **essence of Hawaii – geographic isolation** and the **trade winds.** When the first edition sold out, we were forced to make a decision: to simply reprint it or to rewrite it. With an abundance of new information accumulated over the past five years, it was an easy decision to make. The result is this much expanded and much more extensively illustrated *"updated edition"*.

When one focuses on something, information has a way of streaming in. Our detailed research on the beaches of the islands of Kauai and Hawaii and on the ancient lithified sand dunes of Mahaulepu along the southeastern corner of Kauai has given us a much better understanding of the geologic origins of the Hawaiian Islands in general. Association with geologists such as Don Swanson, Scientist-in-Charge of the U.S. Geological Survey(USGS), Hawaii Volcano Observatory on Hawaii Island, Rick Grigg, Professor of Oceanography at the University of Hawaii at Manoa, Robin Holcomb of the USGS and University of Washington, and Michael Garcia of the Department of Geology and Geophysics at the University of Hawaii-Manoa has inspired us. They enhanced our efforts to gather and present a lot of new geological information on Kauai and the rest of the Hawaiian Archipelago. We are greatly indebted to these and the other scientists and researchers mentioned below. The landmark 2002 American Geophysical Union publication *Hawaiian Volcanoes: deep underwater perspectives*, edited by Takahashi and others, provided valuable information from the relatively recent research on the submarine portion of the volcanic mountain-islands of Hawaii. It's the kind of information that is absolutely necessary for a comprehensive vision of the origin of these immense features. We were fortunate to have the results of that research available to us for use in thinking about illustrations for this book, especially the geologic stages diagram (Fig. 18).

Many others have assisted us. Robin Holcomb provided illustrations on the bathymetry of the sea floor surrounding the main Hawaiian Islands (Fig. 15) and the geology of the sea floor around Kauai (Fig. 34). Barry Eakins of the USGS, Menlo Park, CA contributed the skillfully compiled and edited image of the sea floor surrounding Kauai and Niihau (Fig. 33). Peter Mouginis-Mark of the School of Ocean and Earth Science and Technology (SOEST), University of Hawaii-Manoa took the time to generate, specifically for our book, the beautiful, revealing high-angle oblique relief-satellite photo images of Kauai (Figs. 26 and 27). Dan Walker of the Tsunami Memorial Institute, Oahu, and George Curtis, University of Hawaii-Hilo, assisted us with information and illustrations dealing with tsunamis that have impacted Hawaii over the past century (Figs 22 and 23). Don Swanson, Rick Grigg, and Mike Garcia, along with Scott Rowland of the Hawaii Institute of Geophysics and Planetology, SOEST, University of Hawaii-Manoa and Floyd McCoy of the Geology Department at Windward Community College on Oahu all provided valuable editorial review of the comprehensive geologic stages diagram (Fig. 18). Roy Taogoshi of the Water Resources Division of the U.S. Geological Survey, Lihue, Kauai kindly provided the rainfall data for the gauging station at the summit of Mt. Waialeale (Fig. 40). It was certainly a joy to finally be able to document that data in a more precise manner. Anita Manning and DeSoto Brown of the Bishop Museum, Honolulu, were of considerable assistance in debunking the myth of Mark Twain's reference to Waimea Canyon as "The Grand Canyon of the Pacific". That really bothered us for years. It was so nice to be able to put it to rest. You'll read about all of that in our discussion on Waimea Canyon (p. 57-59). Close to the completion of the manuscript Nancy Jones, educational specialist, Quincy, CA assisted us with editorial discussions on the use of words and phrases. Again, thanks to all of you for your contributions.

A couple more things need to me noted here. They fall into the category of **"as soon as something is published it is in danger of being out of date"**. After sending our manuscript off to the printer we became aware of a publication that challenged one of the oldest and most generally accepted concepts dealing with the origin of the Hawaiian-Emperor volcanic mountain chain, a **fixed** magmatic hotspot. A paper in *Science* by Tarduno et al., 2003 presents the conclusion that, based on paleomagnetic and radiometric age data from samples recovered by ocean drilling, the Emperor Seamount trend was principally formed by the **rapid motion** of the Hawaiian hotspot plume 81 to 47 millions years ago. Earth scientists will be sorting that out over the next few years. During the last week of 2003 an oceanographic cruise was conducted to map the seafloor close-in around Kauai and Niihau. Preliminary results of that survey indicate, among many other things, that the famous escarpment of **Na Pali** was created mainly by **wave erosion** (Brian Taylor, SOEST, personal communication, 2003). As stated many places in this book, since the late 1980s most earth scientists have thought that the north-facing sea cliffs were a result initially of catastrophic structural failure of Kauai's shield volcanic mass. Science is beautiful. It keeps us hypothesizing and testing. Stay tuned for the results of future thought and research.

INTRODUCTION

Kauai and the rest of the Hawaiian Islands are geologically, geographically and biologically unique. **The 132 islands, reefs and shoals** that comprise the **State of Hawaii** extend **for nearly 1600 miles** from the "Big Island" of Hawaii on the southwest to Kure Atoll at the northwestern end of the archipelago. These dots of land are the **Earth's most isolated islands**, lying in the middle of the North Pacific Ocean some 2400 miles from both the nearest continental land mass, North America, and other islands of Polynesia in the South Pacific Ocean. **The islands of Hawaii were one of the last places on Earth occupied by humans.** There is little or no direct evidence of human contact of any kind before about 300 AD. The first significant colonies, made by ocean voyaging Polynesians, were not established until around AD 400-600. Such was due to Hawaii's geographic location, itself a direct result of its **geologic uniqueness**.

Hawaii is a place where **the main elements of the Earth's surface and subsurface** interact in a dynamic, and often dramatic, fashion. As new earth has been created by the volcanic production of the Hawaiian mountain-islands above the floor of the Pacific Ocean, and eventually above sea level, the **lithosphere** (land) has been brought into contact with the **hydrosphere** (ocean) and **atmosphere** (air). Subsequently, prior to the appearance of humans, a unique portion of the Earth's **biosphere** developed as plants and animals migrated to and evolved on these severely isolated islands. Over 4,300 species of Hawaii's land plants and animals (including 2,300 insects and 1,000 land snails) exist only in the eight high Hawaiian Islands. Scientists refer to such species as **"endemic"**. The parent species from which these endemic species evolved somehow migrated to the present islands, or to pre-existing islands of the Hawaiian-Emperor Volcanic Chain, across more than 2,000 miles of open ocean, many with the help of birds. Not surprisingly, no flightless land mammals are endemic to Hawaii. A single species of bat and the monk seal, which do spend some of their time on land, are the only known mammals. Again, the geologic/geographic setting has been the ultimate controlling element.

This book deals mainly with aspects of that portion of the Earth's lithosphere occupied by the Hawaiian Islands, and even more specifically with the geologic history of the Island of Kauai. The book is organized loosely into four related portions. By design, only a small amount of text is provided. Many illustrations are modifications of key technical diagrams derived from the geologic literature. The captions have been simplified and expanded to enhance their impact. The first portion of the book (illustrations on pages 7-34) provides an overview of the character and origin of the greater Hawaiian volcanic mountain-island system, which

1

has been produced over the past 75-80 million years as the Pacific Tectonic Plate moved over the Hawaiian Magmatic Hot Spot. A second portion (illustrations on pages 37-56) deals specifically with Kauai's geologic history and aspects of the Earth's atmospheric circulation that have produced the trade winds and extreme amount of rain fall at Mt. Waialeale near the center of the island. That is followed, on pages 60-87, by illustrations of the several special places on Kauai (Waimea Canyon, Mahaulepu Coast and Na Pali) and an overview of the character and origin of the island's beautiful sandy beaches. A final illustration, the Kauai/Earth Time Line (page 89), and the Concluding Remarks present various aspects of Kauai, and the Hawaiian Islands in general, within a framework of the 10 orders of magnitude of geologic time.

KEY POINTS
The following is a list of key points illustrated by this book.

1. The eight main **high islands** of the Hawaiian Archipelago include Hawaii, Maui, Oahu, Kauai, Molokai, Lanai, Niihau and Kahoolawe (listed in order of size). They occupy, at the southeast end, only about **350 miles** of the nearly 1600 mile long Hawaiian Islands chain, and range in geologic age from **less than 0.5 million years** (oldest portion of the island of Hawaii) successively to only slightly **greater than 5.0 million years** (Kauai and Niihau). These eight islands make up over 99 percent of the 6,425 square miles of land area of the state of Hawaii. They include some of the **Earth's largest mountains**, rising from oceanic depths of greater than 18,000 feet to a height above sea level of nearly 14,000 feet, in the case of Mauna Kea on the Big Island of Hawaii. That's a mountain with relief of 32,000 feet.

2. The entire **Hawaiian-Emperor Volcanic Chain**, which extends for **3570 miles** across the North Pacific Ocean, actually comprises more than **107 individual volcanic mountains**. The tops of most no longer rise above sea level to form islands. They range from the eight high volcanic islands (which comprise portions of at least 15 of those volcanic mountains), to the northwestern low volcanic islands and coral atoll type islands, and to an extensive chain of submerged oceanic mountains (now called **"seamounts"**). Kauai, the oldest of the high islands, is only slightly greater than 5.0 million years old. The low islands to the northwest, 480 to 1525 miles away from the Kilauea volcanic crater on Hawaii Island, are successively older to around **28 million years at Midway**. The submerged **Emperor Seamounts** extend on as far north as the North Pacific Aleutian Submarine Trench where they are greater than **70 million years old**.

3. Based on extensive geologic dating it has been determined that the **average rate of propagation of the Hawaiian-Emperor Volcanic Chain has been 3.4 inches/year** (8.6 cm/yr). That is, the volcanic chain has been formed by the growth of volcanic ocean mountains as the Earth's **Pacific Tectonic Plate** moved across **the Hawaiian Magmatic Hot Spot** at a rate of three and a half inches per year. The plate is still moving at that rate.

4. About **40-43 million years ago, a change in the direction of movement** of the Pacific Tectonic Plate, from northward to northwestward, resulted in the **dog leg bend** in the Hawaiian-Emperor Volcanic Chain. That change is thought to be related to the separation of the Australian and Indian tectonic plates from Antarctica, subsequent movement northward and the eventual **collision of the Indian Plate with Asia** to form the Himalayan Mountains.

5. Most of the volcanic mountain-island systems of the Hawaiian-Emperor Chain have evolved through several **discernible geologic stages of growth, emergence, decline and submergence**. The many stages can be grouped into two major phases; 1) the **dominantly constructive phase** (1-1.5 million years long) during which time the volcanic mountain grows from its submarine stage to its subaerial shield-building stage, and 2) the **dominantly destructive phase** (75-80 million years long) during which the mountain-islands subside, weather and erode as they move along with the tectonic plate until they are subducted back into the Earth's upper mantle.

6. The volcanic mountain-islands have undergone extensive destruction by **large scale subsidence, structural failure** (e.g., central collapse and marginal slumps) and **mass wasting** of submarine slopes, including giant landslides that extend out away from many of the islands for up to over 100 miles. The spectacular sea cliffs along the northern portion of Molokai and the Napali coast of Kauai represent, in part, giant fault scarps resulting from such structural failures. Extensive **atmospheric erosion**, which has formed deep river valleys, and moderate to extensive **oceanic shoreline erosion** also have helped reduce the size of the islands by the removal of sedimentary products to the surrounding deep ocean floor.

7. Kauai, the oldest of the eight major high Hawaiian Islands, displays most of the products of the processes of the dominantly **constructive and destructive phases** operating on these mid-ocean volcanic mountain-islands. The four volcanic rock members of the Waimea Canyon Basalt represent the bulk of the island. The shield-building phase is represented mainly by the **Napali Member** (age 5.10-4.35 my), which is particularly well displayed in the Napali sea cliffs. The post-shield phase, which began with massive collapse along the Waimea Canyon fault scarp, included eruption of the **Olokele Member** (age to 3.95 my) and the graben-filling **Makaweli Member** (age 4.16-3.92 my). Rejuvenation stage volcanism resulted in the production of lavas and explosive volcanic vents of the **Koloa Volcanics** (age 3.65-0.52 my) which cover, like a thin veneer, most of the eastern half of the island.

8. Kauai's glorious **climate** is a result of the location of the Hawaiian Islands at the margins of the tropics and inside a **belt of persistent trade winds**. The **phenomenon of Mt. Waialeale**, one of the rainiest locations on Earth, is a product of the structural development of a cliff that faces the prevailing trade winds. That combination has produced perhaps the planet's perfect **"rain machine"**.

9. The production of calcareous sediments (i.e., calcium-carbonate skeletal deposits), mainly within the fringing **coral/algal reef** systems and other shoreline sedimentary environments such as the **sandy beaches**,

continues to add to the island of Kauai. However, continued **slow subsidence** of the mountain-island and destructive **erosional processes** within the atmosphere and hydrosphere are destroying the island at a significant rate, geologically speaking. Within another 2 to 3 million years Kauai will be reduced to nothing more than a low island, similar to the islands of Nihoa or Necker, incapable of supporting a diversified flora and fauna.

      10. All **geomorphic features** and local climatic aspects of Kauai can be explained in terms of the geologic history of the island. Examples include; **a)** the fault scarp that initiated the erosion of **Waimea Canyon**, **b)** the fault scarp resulting in portions of the spectacular sea cliffs of the **Napali Coast**, **c)** collapse of the eastern portion of the island to produce the **Lihue Basin**, and **d)** the eastern-facing fault scarp of **Mt. Waialeale**, across which dramatic orographic lifting of warm, moist, trade wind-driven air results in one of the rainiest places on Earth.

Hawaiian Archipelago / Volcanic-Mountain Chain
Isolated on the Planet's Largest Geoconveyor Belt

This book deals principally with the island of Kauai; however, in order to set the stage, the initial group of illustrations are provided to gradually bring you to the realization that Kauai is just one island of many within the Hawaiian Archipelago that have evolved in a complex manner and are moving slowly to the northwest on the Earth's largest oceanic tectonic plate. We here in Hawaii live on the planet's largest **"geoconveyor belt"**.

Geographic isolation, one of the most essential aspects of Hawaii, is a result of the volcanic growth of the **planet's largest mountains** in the middle of the ocean of the **Pacific Tectonic Plate.** As the oceanic crustal plate has moved across **The Hawaiian Hot Spot** (a large plume-like source of molten lava rising from the upper mantle) huge volcanoes have been created. Many of the volcanoes not only make it to sea level (a distance of 18,000 feet up) but grow to over 10,000 feet above it. The **plate's movement** is relatively slow, about **3 to 4 inches/year,** but that's fast enough to produce a long chain of mountains with beautiful island tops that string out across the North Pacific Ocean. The islands of the Hawaiian Archipelago stretch for nearly **1600 miles,** from Hawaii Island on the southeast to the atolls of Midway and Kure. Now, 3 to 4 inches/year isn't fast in human years, but in terms of volcano years it's fast. Our **fingernails grow** only at the rate of about **1-1.5 inches/year,** so we can at least say that the islands are moving over twice as fast as that. The **main eight high islands** of Hawaii, which span about **350 miles,** have been strung out across the "geoconveyor" in the past **5 million years,** that also being the age of Kauai (oldest of the bunch).

One of the **basic things** that earth scientists have discovered about Hawaii's volcanic mountain-islands, and keep rediscovering, is that they each are born, grow, mature, and die, and are reabsorbed eventually into the planet in a complex but recognizably repeatable manner. In fact, a number of **geologic stages** have been delineated to help track the steps through which the mountains evolve as the plate on which they reside moves. We have emphasized **two basic groups** of these stages (Fig. 18); 1) the **dominantly constructive** phase and 2) the **dominantly destructive** phase. The dominantly **constructive phase** involves **growth of the volcanic mountain** from a submarine stage through its subaerial (i.e., above sea level) shield-building stage. The rapidly growing mountain does suffer frequent and severe catastrophic structural failure (e.g., down faulting) during this growth period; however, overall it is still growing. All of that takes only about **1 - 1.5 million years.** The dominantly **destructive phase,** which continues over the subsequent **75 - 80 million years,** involves continued plate tectonic movement, subsidence, weathering and erosion in which the Earth **recycles** the mountain through its atmosphere and hydrosphere back into its upper mantle. **Hawaii is a dynamic place.**

6

PACIFIC BASIN LOCATION

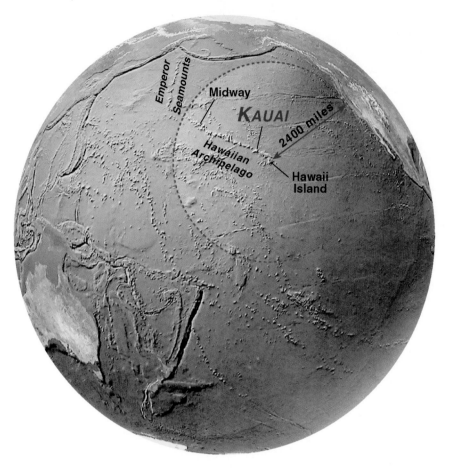

(modified from Pernetta, 1994)

FIGURE 1. **Geographic isolation** may be the most significant aspect of the Hawaiian Islands. Located in the middle of the North Pacific Ocean, islands of the Hawaiian Archipelago constitute the **Earth's most isolated major land mass**. The nearest continent of North America and island chains of Polynesia are at distances of **over 2400 miles**. Portions of Asia and Australia are over 3500 miles distant. The genetically related chain of volcanic mountains of the **Hawaiian Archipelago and Emperor Seamounts** extends for over **3200 miles** northwestward and then northward to the junction of the **Aleutian and Kuril ocean trenches.** Such trenches represent tectonic plate subduction zones. Note also the linear trend of other islands/seamount chains of Polynesia, the prominent fracture zones extending across the North Pacific Ocean Basin, and other oceanic trenches along western portions of the ocean basin.

7

PACIFIC RIM DISTANCES

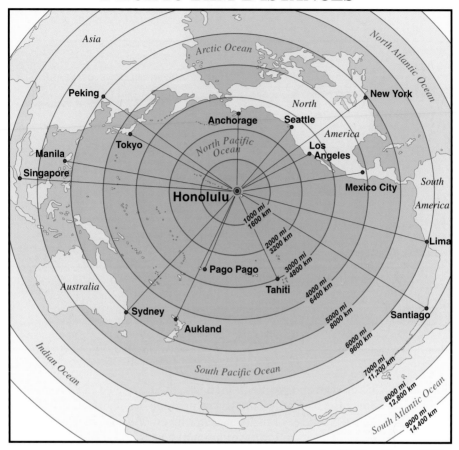

(modified from Graves, 1983)

FIGURE 2. It appears a bit distorted. That's the way it is with two-dimensional projections of three-dimensional objects. However, this **equidistant projection** of the globe with **Honolulu near the center of the Pacific Rim**, like one of the poles of the earth, provides an accurate vision of **the isolation of the Hawaiian Islands**. Note that **North America** is by far the **closest major land mass**. The **Asian continent**, from which many of the **founding species of plants and insects** arrived in the islands via birds, high altitude winds and ocean currents is 4000+ miles distant. **Islands of Polynesia**, from which the **first human inhabitants** arrived around 1500 years ago (+/- 300 yrs) via ocean navigation, are around 3000 miles away. In addition to its continuing influence on the natural elements of Hawaii, isolation is a major factor in terms of the many facets of the island's **politics** and **economy**.

HAWAIIAN ARCHIPELAGO

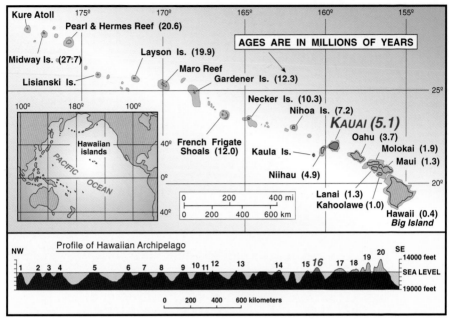

[modified from Macdonald, et al. (1983), as modified from Stearns (1946)]

FIGURE 3. Classic map and profile of high islands and related low island features of the **Hawaiian Volcanic Island Archipelago**. Emphasized is the submerged and eroded character of the islands northwest of Kauai, many of which are capped by reef deposits to form various atoll type island complexes. These volcanic mountain-islands start as much as 18,000 feet below sea level and extend to as much as 14,000 feet above sea level. Numbers in parentheses indicate average absolute ages (in millions of years) of the various volcanic mountain-island features, as determined by geologic dating techniques.

Features indicated by numbers in the lower profile view are as follows:

1. Kure Island	12. French Frigate Shoals
2. Midway Islands	& La Perouse Rocks
3. Gambia Shoal	13. Necker Island
4. Pearl & Hermes Reef	14. Nihoa Island
5. Fisher Reef & Neva Shoal	15. Niihau
6. Laysan Island	16. *KAUAI*
7. Maro Reef	17. Oahu
8. Raita Bank	18. Molokai
9. Gardner Island	19. Maui
10. St. Rogatien Bank	20. Hawaii
11. Brooks Bank	

THE ISLANDS OF THE STATE OF HAWAII

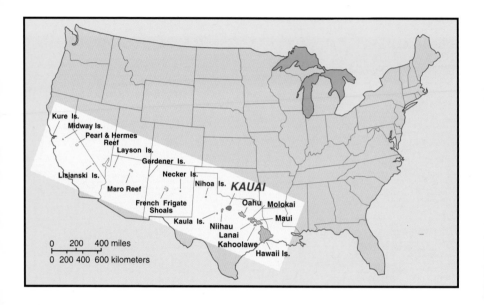

FIGURE 4. The 132 islands, reefs and shoals that make up the **State of Hawaii** are shown here superimposed at the same scale over the contiguous 48 states. They stretch across the central North Pacific Ocean for nearly 1600 miles (2560 km), equivalent to the distance from western Louisiana to San Francisco. The **eight main high islands** at the southeastern end of the archipelago span a distance of only about 350 miles. Seven of the high islands (excepting Kahoolawe) and Midway Atoll to the far northwest, are the only islands inhabited by humans on a regular basis. Most of the **northwestern islands** are under the jurisdiction of the U.S. Fish and Wildlife Service and occupied mainly by insects, seabirds and the sparse and endangered Hawaiian monk seal.

HAWAIIAN ISLANDS SPACE PHOTO
(EIGHT MAIN HIGH ISLANDS)

FIGURE 5. The eight main **high islands** of Hawaii extend for over **350 miles** (565 km) from the active volcano of Kilauea on the "Big Island" of Hawaii to the "Forbidden Island" of Niihau. This space photo, with the curvature of the Earth displayed in the background, shows the relative distribution of these islands. Note the **cloud patterns** on the islands, with north and eastern portions of Kauai, Oahu, Molokai and West Maui covered by clouds. Such patterns are produced by **orographic lifting** and cooling of warm, moist **trade wind** driven air. The high altitude portions of Hawaii Island and East Maui (Haleakala Volcano) are clear (above 8,000 ft) due to the **trade wind inversion layer**, above which moisture is very low. The 100 mile distance between Oahu and Kauai is the greatest distance between any of these main islands resulting in Kauai's common label as **"The Separate Kingdom"**.

HAWAIIAN VOLCANIC MOUNTAIN-ISLAND CHAIN

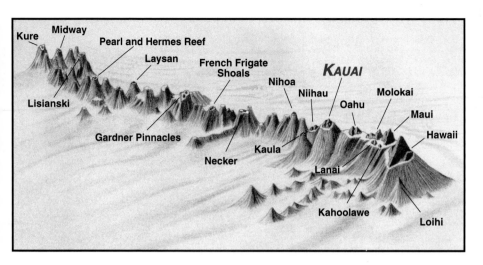

FIGURE 6. The **Hawaiian Archipelago** extends across the middle of the North Pacific Ocean for nearly **1600 miles** (>2500 km), a distance measured from the presently active volcano of Kilauea on Hawaii Island northwestward to the atolls of Midway and Kure. As viewed in this artistic, water-removed illustration, the **above sea level** portion of the various **132** islands, reefs and shoals of the State of Hawaii represent **less than 2.5%** of the volume occupied by the huge volcanic mountains. **More than 97.5% of Hawaii is underwater!** Numerous seamounts (i.e., sea mountains) also are present in this portion of the ocean with water depths extending to 18,000 ft (5,500 meters). The **eight main high islands** of Hawaii make up over **99%** of the 6,435 square miles of Hawaii's land area. The above water portion of Hawaii Island represents 11% of the volume of the five volcanoes that comprise its mountain-island complex. **Loihi Seamount**, located about 20 miles (30 km) south of Kilauea Volcano, is the newest active Hawaiian volcanic mountain. Its summit is at **3180 ft** (970 meters) below sea level, but its base is at 15,500 ft (4,755 meters), making it a **12,320 ft** (3,755 meter) mountain.

Also it is worth noting that the Hawaiian Lexicon Committee recently has identified **Hawaiian names** for the following places of the **Northwestern Hawaiian Islands**:

Necker Is. - *Mokumanamana*   Lisianski Is. - *Papa`apoho*
French Frigate Shoals - *Mokupapapa*   Pearl and Hermes Atoll - *Holoikauaua*
Gardner Pinnacles - *Puhahonu*   Midway Atoll - *Pihemanu*
Maro Reef - *Nalukakala*   Kure Atoll - *Kanemiloha`i*
Laysan Is. - *Kauo*

HAWAIIAN-EMPEROR VOLCANIC CHAIN

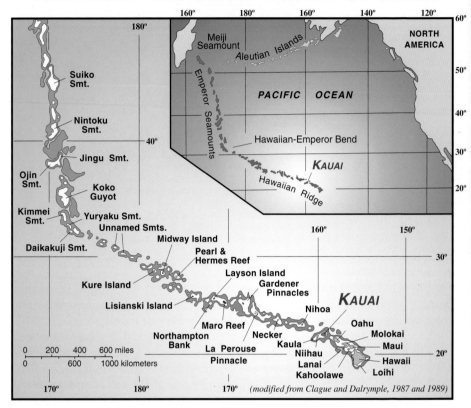

<u>FIGURE 7.</u> The Hawaiian Archipelago and Emperor Seamounts are genetically related volcanic mountains, commonly referred to as the **Hawaiian-Emperor Volcanic Chain.** This extensive mountain system, one of the world's longest, formed as the **Pacific Tectonic Plate** moved northward and then northwestward across the **Hawaiian Magmatic Hot Spot** in the central North Pacific Ocean. More than **107 individual volcanoes** have been delineated within the **3570 mile** (5750 km) long chain; the Hawaiian Island-Seamount Chain (to the bend) is 2140 miles (3450 km); the Emperor Seamount Chain adds 1430 miles (2300 km). Islands and seamount systems are delineated here by 1- and 2-km depth contours; average depth of the ocean floor in the Hawaiian Island region is 3 mi (5 km). Significant **absolute ages** (<u>in millions of years</u>) of selected islands and seamounts include: Hawaii Island, 0-0.4; **Kauai, 5.1;** Midway Islands (including Kure Is.), 27.7; Koko Seamount, 50.6; Kimmel and Daikakuji Seamounts (at bend), 47.3-46.7; Suiko Seamount, 61.3-64.7; Meiji Seamount, approximately 75-80. The **change in the direction** of movement of the Pacific Tectonic Plate beginning about **50 million years ago** is thought to be related to the collision of India with Asia to produce the Himalayan Mountains and other tectonic features at the boundary of the Asian and the Indo-Australian tectonic plates.

HAWAIIAN-EMPEROR VOLCANIC MOUNTAIN CHAIN

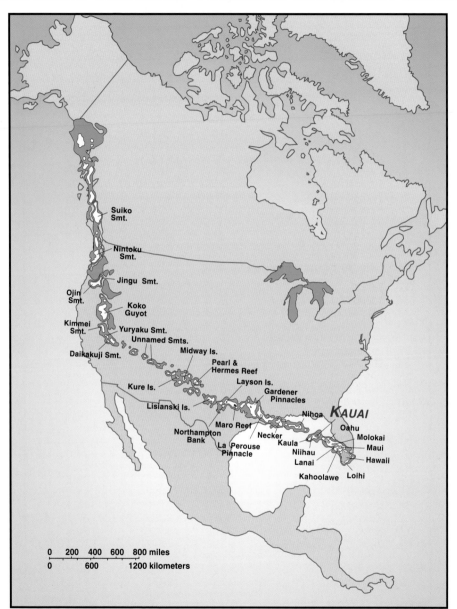

FIGURE 8. Although mostly underwater, and difficult to visualize, the aligned **Hawaiian-Emperor Volcanic Mountain Chain** covers a significant portion of the Earth's surface. **It is one of planet's longest mountain chain**. When superimposed, at the same scale, over the North American continent it extends northwestward from Miami to near Reno and then north through Seattle to the panhandle of Alaska, a distance of nearly 3600 miles (5750 kilometers).

ABSOLUTE GEOLOGIC AGES

Volcano No. Name		Distance from Kilauea		Radiometric Age (K-Ar)
High Hawaiian Islands:		Kilometers	(Miles)	(Millions of Years)
1	Kilauea ⎤ Big Island	0		0-0.4
3	Mauna Kea ⎬ Big Island	54	(34)	0.375
5	Kohala ⎦	100	(62)	0.43
6	East Maui	182	(113)	0.75
7	Kahoolawe	185	(115)	1.03
8	West Maui ⎬ Maui Nui	221	(137)	1.32
9	Lanai	226	(140)	1.28
10	East Molokai	256	(159)	1.76
11	West Molokai ⎦	280	(174)	1.90
12	Koolau ⎬ Oahu	339	(210)	2.6
13	Waianae ⎦	374	(232)	3.7
14	*KAUAI*	*519*	*(322)*	*5.1*
15	Niihau	565	(351)	4.9
Northwestern Low Hawaiian Islands:				
17	Nihoa	780	(484)	7.2
20	unnamed	913	(567)	9.6
23	Necker	1058	(657)	10.3
26	La Perouse Pinnacle *(French Frigates Shoals)*	1209	(751)	12.0
27	Brooks Bank	1256	(800)	13.0
30	Gardner Pinnacles	1435	(891)	12.3
36	Laysan	1818	(1129)	19.9
37	Northampton Bank	1841	(1143)	26.6
50	Pearl & Hermes Reef	2291	(1432)	20.6
52	Midway Islands	2432	(1510)	27.7
Emperor Seamounts:				
57	unnamed	2600	(1615)	28.0
63	unnamed	2825	(1754)	27.4
65	Colahan	3128	(1942)	**38.8***
65a	Abbott	3280	(2037)	**41.5***
67	Daikakuji	3493	(2169)	**46.7***
72	Kimmei	3668	(2285)	**47.3***
74	Koko	3758	(2334)	**50.6***
81	Ojin	4102	(2547)	55.2
83	Jingu	4175	(2593)	55.4
86	Nintoku	4452	(2765)	56.2
90	Suiko	4794	(2977)	**61.3***
91	Suiko	4860	(3018)	64.7

* new dates from Sharp and Clague, 2002   *(simplified from Clague and Dalrymple, 1989 with update from Sharp and Clague, 2002)*

FIGURE 9. Summary of **absolute geologic ages** of islands and seamounts along the **Hawaiian-Emperor Volcanic Chain**, based on Potassium-Argon (K-Ar) radiometric determinations. Note that **new dates** (in bold with *) have been added for seamounts on either side of the **Hawaiian-Emperor Bend** as a result of the work of Sharp and Clague, 2002.

CROSS-PLOT OF GEOLOGIC AGES OF THE HAWAIIAN-EMPEROR VOLCANIC CHAIN

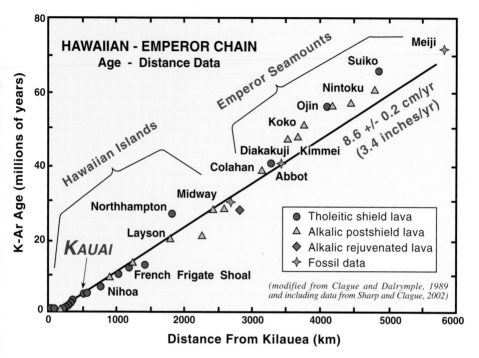

FIGURE 10. Cross-plot of absolute geologic ages of volcanoes in the Hawaiian-Emperor Volcanic Mountain Chain and their distances from the present-day active volcano of Kilauea on the Hawaii Island. The least-squares fit regression of the data (solid line) indicates that the average **rate of propagation** (i.e., speed of movement) **of the Pacific Tectonic Plate across the Hawaiian Magmatic Hot Spot**) for the entire Hawaiian-Emperor chain has been at about **3.4 inches per year** (8.6 cm/yr). Individual shorter segments of the chain indicate slightly slower or faster rates of propagation, ranging from about 2.0-4.5 inch/yr (5.2 to 11.3 cm/yr). Recently Sharp and Clague (2002) provided more accurate geologic dates of the seamounts on either side of the Hawaiian-Emperor Bend and noted that; 1) volcanism migrated at about 10 cm/year (3.9 inches/year) during formation of the southern Emperor Chain, and 2) through the bend migration of volcanism slowed to 5.2 cm/year (2.05 inches/year). Such a change seems consistent with a **fixed** Hawaiian Hot Spot and a nearly **60 degree change in the direction of movement** of the Pacific Tectonic Plate from nearly northward to northwestward around **50 million years ago**.

HIGH ISLANDS OF HAWAII
(PRIMARY VOLCANOES)

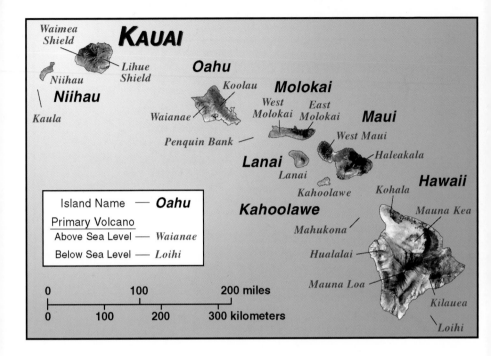

FIGURE 11. Geographic **names** in Hawaii can be confusing. This illustration, with **photographic images** of each island is provided to delineate the **major geographic features** of the main eight high islands of Hawaii. Each of the islands is comprised of portions of one or more volcanoes. Hawaii island also encompasses, to some extent, two seamounts; Mahukona is extinct and submerged, Loihi is active and growing. Penquin Bank is the submerged southwestern rift-zone extension of the West Molokai Volcano. The Kaula Volcano is a relatively small submerged shield south of Niihau; only a very small cinder cone (Kaula Island) is emergent 551 feet above sea level.

HAWAIIAN MOUNTAIN/ISLAND HEIGHTS

Volcano	Present Height		Maximum Height		Age
Big Island	Meters	(Feet)	Meters	(Feet)	(Millions of Years)
Loihi	- 950	(-3,116)	- 950	(-3,116)	no data
Kilauea	1,247	(4,090)	1,247	(4,090)	0-0.4
Mauna Loa	4,169	(13,674)	4,169	(13,674)	0-0.4
Mauna Kea	4,205	(13,792)	4,600	(15,088)	0.38
Hualalai	2,521	(8,269)	2,950	(9,676)	no data
Kohala	1,670	(5,478)	2,670	(8,758)	0.43
Mahukona	-1,100	(-3,608)	235	(771)	no data
Maui Nui					
Haleakala	3,055	(10,020)	5,000	(16,400)	0.75
Kahoolawe	450	(1,476)	2,100	(6,888)	1.03
West Maui	1,764	(5,786)	3,300	(10,824)	1.76
Lanai	1,027	(3,369)	2,200	(7,216)	1.28
East Molokai	1,515	(4,969)	3,300	(10,824)	1.76
West Molokai	421	(1,381)	1,600	(5,248)	1.9
Penquin Bank	- 200	(- 656)	1,000	(3,280)	no data
Oahu					
Koolau	960	(3,149)	1,900	(6,232)	2.6
Waianae	1,231	(4,038)	2,200	(7,216)	3.7
KAUAI	*1,598*	*(5,243)*	*2,600*	*(8,528)*	*5.1*
Niihau	390	(1,279)	1,400	(4,592)	4.9
Kaula	168	(551)	800	(2,624)	4.0
Outer Islands					
Nihoa	277	(909)	1,300	(4,264)	7.2
Necker	84	(275)	1,100	(3,608)	10.3

(modified from Carson and Clague, 1995)

FIGURE 12. Summary of **present heights** (or depths below sea level), **previous maximum heights**, and **absolute geologic ages** of the present major **Hawaiian volcanoes**. Note that **Kauai** has subsided (sunk) over 3000 feet (1000 meters) since its volcanic origin over 5 million years ago.

SUBAERIAL VOLCANO BUILDING STAGES
HIGH ISLANDS OF HAWAII

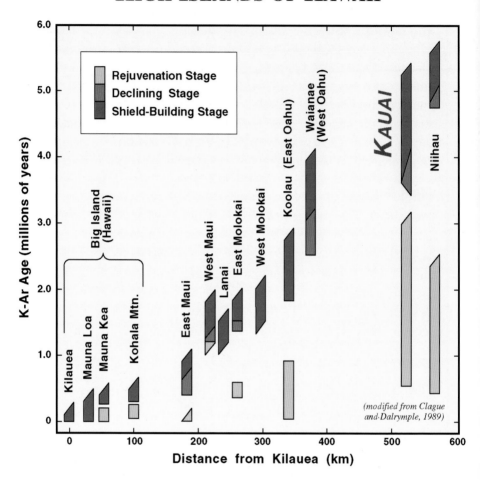

FIGURE 13. The main high islands of Hawaii display three major stages of volcano building, including: **1)** the initial, major, **shield-building stage** (red), **2)** a minor **post-shield (or declining) stage** (blue), and **3)** the final **rejuvenation stage** (yellow). Such determinations have been based on extensive analysis of the geologic character (i.e., distribution and chemical/mineralogical analysis) of the main volcanic rock formations on each island. Known durations of the three **major above-sea level stages of volcano building** recognized for the main high islands of Hawaii are displayed here plotted against the distance from the active Kilauea volcano on Hawaii Island.

EARTHQUAKES IN HAWAII
(1962-1980, MAGNITUDE > 3.0)

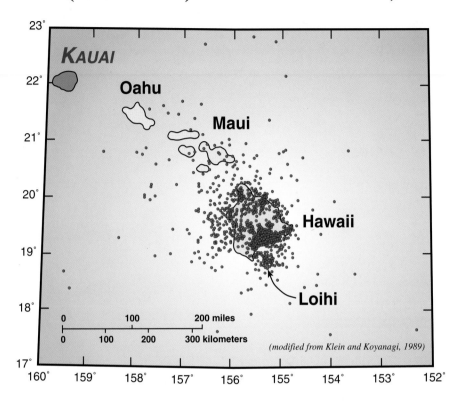

FIGURE 14. Earthquakes in Hawaii result mainly from a) the **injection of molten magma** through the oceanic crust into a growing volcanic mountain and b) **landslides** of unstable mountain slopes. The magma rises from the earth's mantle and lower crust and is injected through the upper crust to create the Hawaiian, mid-ocean volcanic mountain masses. Landslides, both above and below sea level, are a result of the instability of the slopes of the rapidly growing volcanoes. A plot of all earthquakes with magnitude greater than 3.0 (on the Richter scale) for the years 1962-1984 revealed a **general concentration of seismic activity around Hawaii Island**, and especially in the vicinity of the Kilauea and Loihi volcanic structures. The plot of earthquakes for any 20 year period would display a similar concentration. This distribution is indicative of the **magmatic "hot spot"** mainly below **Hawaii Island and Loihi**. Loihi is the new submarine volcanic mountain of Hawaii with its summit 3180 feet below sea level. It is actively growing 20 miles (30 km) south of Kilauea, presenting more evidence of the continued **northwestward movement of the Pacific Tectonic Plate across the stationary Hawaiian Hot Spot**.

HAWAII SEA FLOOR
SIDE SCAN SONAR IMAGE

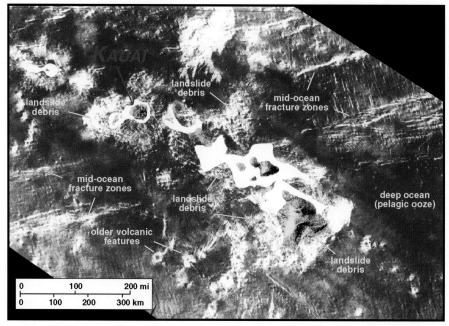

(courtesy of Robin Holcomb)

FIGURE 15. **Side scan sonar image** of the sea floor surrounding the main high islands of Hawaii. Blank areas near islands could not be surveyed owing to shallow depths. Smooth, relatively flat areas of the ocean floor (dark areas) range up to **18,000 feet** deep in the North Pacific Basin. Prominent east-west trending lineaments are **mid-ocean fracture zones** that extend across most of the ocean basin. The light mottled areas surrounding the volcanic mountain-islands are **gigantic landslides** composed of **avalanche debris** that moved down the submarine slope of the shield mountain during **catastrophic structural failure**. Some of the fan-shaped piles of chaotic landslide material contain upturned blocks several miles in length. Such deposit can extend for over a hundred miles away from the mountain source. Most major landslide events occur during the early, **constructive phase of volcano building**. The volcanic mountain builds itself **too high too fast** resulting in instability. Catastrophic failure in the form of gigantic slumps is evidenced mainly by the chaotic fabric and fan shapes of the deposits.

SUBMARINE LANDSLIDES OF MAIN HAWAIIAN ISLANDS

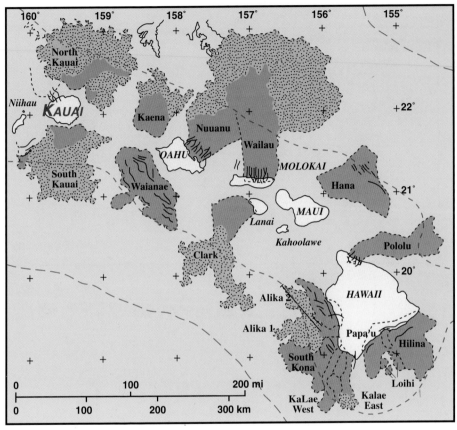

(modified from Moore, et al., 1989)

FIGURE 16. Map of the **southeastern Hawaiian Volcanic Ridge** showing the location of the eight major high islands of Hawaii and the **submarine landslides, debris flow deposits** and related features surrounding the various volcanic mountain complexes. Patterns are based mainly on **side-scan sonar surveys** such as that illustrated in Figure 15. Green patterns indicate the location of **chaotic landslide deposits** composed of large randomly-oriented blocks. The gray stipple represents areas of hummocky submarine **debris flow** and **density current deposits. Fault scarps** at the heads of submarine slides are indicated by hachured lines. Thin downslope lines indicate probable **submarine canyons.** The axis of the **Hawaiian Deep** is indicated by interior dashed red line whereas the crest of the **Hawaiian Arch** is indicated by the outer dashed red line.

SUBMARINE GEOLOGIC DEPOSITS

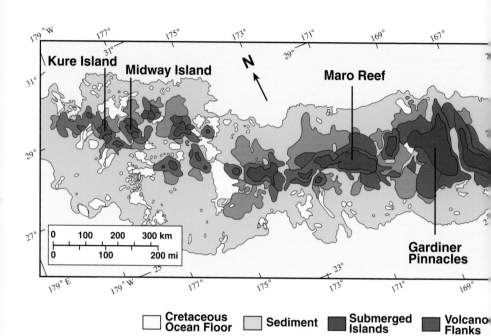

Kure Island Midway Island Maro Reef Gardiner Pinnacles

0   100   200   300 km
0   100   200 mi

□ Cretaceous Ocean Floor   □ Sediment   ■ Submerged Islands   ■ Volcano Flanks

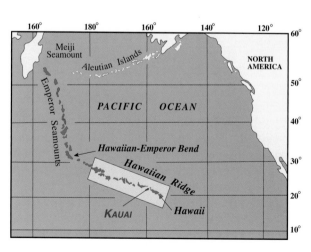

Meiji Seamount Aleutian Islands NORTH AMERICA Emperor Seamounts PACIFIC OCEAN Hawaiian-Emperor Bend Hawaiian Ridge KAUAI Hawaii

SITE LOCATION MAP

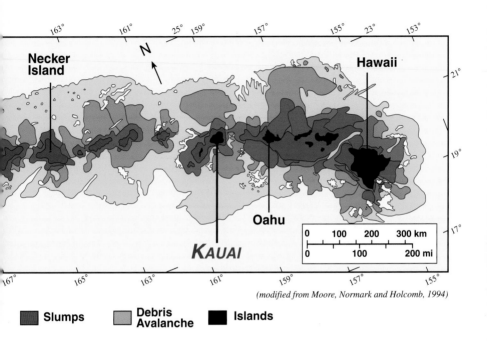

(modified from Moore, Normark and Holcomb, 1994)

■ Slumps　　□ Debris Avalanche　　■ Islands

FIGURE 17. **Submarine geologic deposits** of the Hawaiian Volcanic Chain from Hawaii Island to the Midway and Kure Islands. Of significance are the **submarine slumps, debris flows and redeposited volcanic/carbonate sediments** indicative of the **destructive processes** that affect Hawaiian mid-ocean volcanic mountain/islands. At least **68 major submarine landslides** more than **12.5 mi** (20 km) **long** have been mapped along the stretch of the **Hawaiian Ridge** shown here, which developed over the past **30 million years**. Most large scale landslide deposits probably were created by **catastrophic structural failure** (i.e., faulting and slumping) of **unstable volcanic mountain-islands** as they grew too high too fast early in their development (i.e., within the first 500,000 to 1,000,000 years). Geology of the sea floor has been inferred mainly from the side-looking sonar system **GLORIA** (Geologic Long-Range Inclined Asdic), which records acoustic back-scatter from the seafloor in an effective swath 15-20 mi wide. See example of imagery in Figure 15.

I. Dominantly <u>Constructive</u> Phase (0 - 1,500,000 years)

Submarine Stage
0 - 300,000 years

(e.g. Loihi)

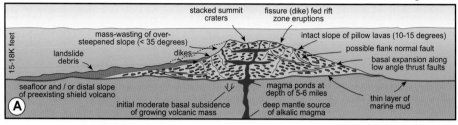

15-18K feet

- stacked summit craters
- fissure (dike) fed rift zone eruptions
- mass-wasting of over-steepened slope (< 35 degrees)
- intact slope of pillow lavas (10-15 degrees)
- landslide debris
- dikes
- possible flank normal fault
- basal expansion along low angle thrust faults
- seafloor and / or distal slope of preexisting shield volcano
- magma ponds at depth of 5-6 miles
- thin layer of marine mud
- (A) initial moderate basal subsidence of growing volcanic mass
- deep mantle source of alkalic magma

Emergent Stage - at approx.
300,000 - 500,000 years

(no present example)

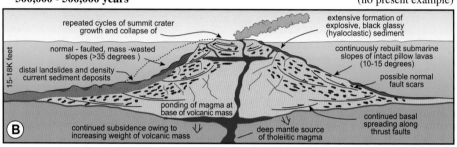

15-18K feet

- repeated cycles of summit crater growth and collapse of
- extensive formation of explosive, black glassy (hyaloclastic) sediment
- normal - faulted, mass -wasted slopes (>35 degrees)
- continuously rebuilt submarine slopes of intact pillow lavas (10-15 degrees)
- distal landslides and density current sediment deposits
- possible normal fault scars
- ponding of magma at base of volcanic mass
- (B) continued subsidence owing to increasing weight of volcanic mass
- deep mantle source of tholeiitic magma
- continued basal spreading along thrust faults

Subaerial, Shield-Building Stage
500,000 - 1,000,000 years

(e.g. Mauna Loa)

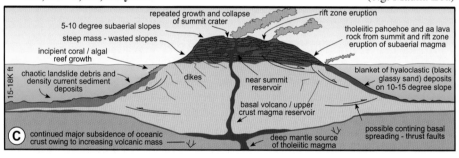

15-18K ft

- repeated growth and collapse of summit crater
- rift zone eruption
- 5-10 degree subaerial slopes
- steep mass - wasted slopes
- tholeiitic pahoehoe and aa lava rock from summit and rift zone eruption of subaerial magma
- incipient coral / algal reef growth
- chaotic landslide debris and density current sediment deposits
- dikes
- near summit reservoir
- blanket of hyaloclastic (black glassy sand) deposits on 10-15 degree slope
- basal volcano / upper crust magma reservoir
- (C) continued major subsidence of oceanic crust owing to increasing volcanic mass
- deep mantle source of tholeiitic magma
- possible contining basal spreading - thrust faults

Declining Stage
1,000,000 - 1,500,000 yrs

(e.g. Mauna Kea)

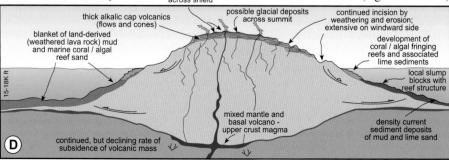

15-18K ft

- scattered cinder cones across shield
- thick alkalic cap volcanics (flows and cones)
- possible glacial deposits across summit
- continued incision by weathering and erosion; extensive on windward side
- blanket of land-derived (weathered lava rock) mud and marine coral / algal reef sand
- development of coral / algal fringing reefs and associated lime sediments
- local slump blocks with reef structure
- (D) continued, but declining rate of subsidence of volcanic mass
- mixed mantle and basal volcano - upper crust magma
- density current sediment deposits of mud and lime sand

25

GEOLOGIC STAGES
HAWAIIAN VOLCANIC MOUNTAIN-ISLANDS

FIGURE 18a. The mid-oceanic shield volcanoes of the Hawaiian-Emperor Volcanic Chain are produced on the Pacific Tectonic Plate as it moves across the Hawaiian Magmatic Hot Spot. During their growth they progress through four recognizable stages (A-D). These stages have been lumped into the **Dominantly Constructive Phase**, during which time the volcanic mountain grows up from the seafloor as much as 18,000 feet to the sea surface and then commonly to over 10,000 feet above sea level. These are the Earth's largest mountains. It takes only 1 to 1.5 million years for their construction. Owing to this rapid rate of growth the huge volcanic structures develop great instability and are subject to massive structural failures which result in prodigious submarine landslides that in some cases extend seaward for over 100 miles. Such failures can be considered destructional events; however, they occur during the overall up building of the volcanic mass. Specific aspects of each of the four stages illustrated to the left are as follows:

A. Submarine Stage (0-300,000+ years) -- The volcano grows up from the seafloor, which may be a relatively flat surface at a depth as great as 18,000 feet; however, more commonly the volcano grows on the inclined flank of a preexisting volcanic mountain at somewhat shallower depth. It may overlie a slippery surface of oceanic mud. It grows by repeated eruption of alkalic magma, which forms relatively intact slopes of pillow lavas as steep as 10-15+ degrees. The rapidly-growing seamount suffers frequent collapse of its summit crater and mass wasting of it over-steepened flanks. The best example of a growing submarine Hawaiian volcano is Loihi, the 2-2.5-mile long summit of which lies at 3,180 feet below sea level. With it's base at about 15,000-16,000 ft below sea level it's already a 12,000-13,000 ft mountain. It should reach the sea surface in another 30,000-50,000 years.

B. Emergent Stage (at approximately 300,000 - 500,000 years) -- The last 200,000+ years of submarine growth is dominated by the increasing eruption of tholeiitic lavas from a relatively deep source of magma in the Earth's upper mantle. The base of the volcanic mass subsides significantly owing to its weight and spreads laterally along probable thrust faults. Structural deformation of its summit craters and submarine flanks continue. As it approaches sea level fragmentation of erupting lava occurs as the magma chills rapidly and violently. That produces large volumes of black glassy (hyaloclastic) sediment which blankets portions of the volcanic mountain's submarine slopes.

C. Subaerial Shield-Building Stage (500,000-1,000,000 years) -- The bulk (over 95%) of the above sea level portion of the volcanic mountain is built during this stage through the effusive (i.e., relatively non-explosive) eruption of tholeiitic lava. Eruptions occur both at summit craters and along extensive lateral rift systems to build the large shield structure with slopes on the order of 5-10 degrees. The massive volcanic mountain subsides. Its base spreads along probable thrust faults. Oversteeping of the mountain flanks continue to result in catastrophic structural failures in which huge masses are down-faulted away in a slump-like manner to produce prodigious submarine landslides. The mountain is the site of frequent earthquakes owing to volcanic eruptions and faulting of unstable flanks.

D. Declining State (1,000,000-1,500,000 years) -- The final stage of volcanic construction produces a cap of alkalic lavas that may extend well across the mountain-island structure, but comprise only less than 1-5% of the volume of the island. Lava erupts both effusively to produce layers of lava and explosively to produce cinder and spatter cones. Across the summit of volcanic mountains that reach heights approaching 14,000 feet (such as Mauna Kea today) glaciers may form to erode and resediment the lava rocks into ground and end moraines. Extensive weathering and erosion breaks down and removes tremendous volumes of lava rock from the mountain as soils form and deep valleys are cut, especially on the windward sides of the island. Biogenic reef structures are built by shallow marine organisms (mainly coral and coralline algae) around the shorelines to form fringing reefs. Reef systems contribute skeletal material to form the famous carbonate sands of the Hawaiian Islands.

II. Dominantly Destructive Phase (1.5 - 80 million years)

Erosional - Rejuvenation Stage
1,500,000 - 4,500,000 yrs

(e.g .Maui - Oahu)

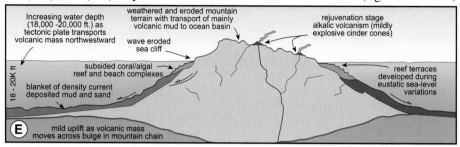

Increasing water depth (18,000 -20,000 ft.) as tectonic plate transports volcanic mass northwestward

weathered and eroded mountain terrain with transport of mainly volcanic mud to ocean basin

wave eroded sea cliff

rejuvenation stage alkalic volcanism (mildly explosive cinder cones)

subsided coral/algal reef and beach complexes

reef terraces developed during eustatic sea-level variations

blanket of density current deposited mud and sand

18 - 20K ft

mild uplift as volcanic mass moves across bulge in mountain chain

E

Late Erosional to Early Atoll Stage
4,500,000 - 12,500,000 yrs

(e.g. **KAUAI** to Gardener Pinnacles)

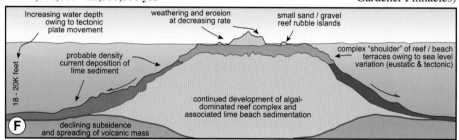

Increasing water depth owing to tectonic plate movement

weathering and erosion at decreasing rate

small sand / gravel reef rubble islands

probable density current deposition of lime sediment

complex "shoulder" of reef / beach terraces owing to sea level variation (eustatic & tectonic)

18 - 20K feet

continued development of algal-dominated reef complex and associated lime beach sedimentation

declining subsidence and spreading of volcanic mass

F

Atoll Stage
12,500,000 - 30,000,000 yrs

(e.g. Brooks Bank to Midway / Kure Atolls)

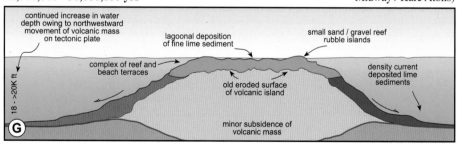

continued increase in water depth owing to northwestward movement of volcanic mass on tectonic plate

lagoonal deposition of fine lime sediment

small sand / gravel reef rubble islands

complex of reef and beach terraces

density current deposited lime sediments

old eroded surface of volcanic island

18 - >20K ft

minor subsidence of volcanic mass

G

Guyot (Seamount) Stage
30,000,000 - 80,000,000 yrs

(e.g. Colahan - Meiji Seamount Chain)

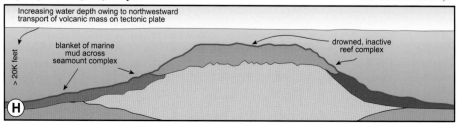

Increasing water depth owing to northwestward transport of volcanic mass on tectonic plate

blanket of marine mud across seamount complex

drowned, inactive reef complex

> 20K feet

H

GEOLOGIC STAGES
HAWAIIAN VOLCANIC MOUNTAIN-ISLANDS

FIGURE 18b. By far the longest phase of the geologic history of the Hawaiian volcanic mountain-islands is the **Dominantly Destructive Phase** which follows the major mountain-building phase and continues for another 75-80 million years. The Pacific Tectonic Plate continues to move the mountains toward their ultimate grave in the subduction zone at the northwestern margin of the Pacific Basin. During this phase there is a minor rejuvenation stage of eruption of cinder and spatter cones, and biogenic reefs continue to develop fringing and ultimately atoll structures; however, overall the mountain is dying. Its height is diminished by subaerial weathering and erosion. Subsidence continues as the weight of the structure depresses the oceanic crust and the tectonic plate slowly drags the mountain into deeper water. Specific aspects of each of the four stages illustrated to the left are as follows:

E. Erosional - Rejuvenation Stage (1.5 - 4.5 million years) -- The subaerial (i.e., island) portion of the high volcanic mountain undergoes extensive weathering and erosion in response to it's interaction with the Earth's atmosphere and hydrosphere. Weathering occurs mainly in the form of oxidation and hydration and is enhanced by plant production of botanical acids. Plants also break rock by rooting. Resultant soil and broken rock is removed by running water. The high islands generate large volumes of water for stream runoff as a result of orographic lifting of the warm, moist trade winds that attack their windward slopes. A relatively minor stage of alkalic-lava volcanic eruption, the Rejuvenation Stage, produces various types of small volcanic features (e.g., lava domes, cinder and spatter cones) which can cover much of the larger shield volcano, but the overall volume is minor. Extensive biogenic reefs develop around the island like a fringe. They are initially composed mainly of coral with grow beginning in nearshore shallow water. As the coral reefs grow to sea level they develop platforms that built seaward. The fringing reef platforms then become dominated by coralline algae which can survive better in the shallow, wave-dominated coastal zones of Hawaii. The coral/algal reefs, interacting with the large high-energy waves of the Pacific Basin, produce most of the sediment that accumulates to form the island's sandy beaches.

F. Late Erosional to Early Atoll State (4.5 - 12.5 million years) -- As the mountain subsides at a decreasing rate, subaerial erosion continues to degrade its island top, although also at a decreasing rate. The diminished island profile produces less rainfall, and therefore less water for stream runoff. However, tremendous volumes of sand and finer sediment is contributed to the sea floor surrounding the dying island, especially early on in this stage. A lush mountain forest system is gradually reduced to low-lying shrub-dominated ecosystems owing to decreasing island height and less and less water being available. The growth of algal-dominated fringing reefs continues as they easily keep up with sea level rise resulting from the sinking of the island. Sandy beaches can be extensive.

G. Atoll Stage (12.5 - 30.0 million years) -- Ultimately volcanic rock succumbs to the sea as it is eaten away by the atmosphere and hydrosphere and pulled under by subsidence. Reefs, still probably dominated by coralline algae, keep up with tectonic sea level rise to grow over the submerged lava rock and keep the island alive as an atoll with its classic high-energy outer reef edge and relatively low-energy inner lagoon. As the reef island is moved into cooler water on the tectonic plate it becomes even more dominated by coralline algae.

H. Seamount Stage (30 - 80 million years) -- Finally the atoll-capped volcanic mass sinks below sea level, owing in part to a decreasing rate of reef growth in the cool North Pacific Ocean water. As it continues its long lonely ride to its ultimate reabsorption at the ocean basin-bounding deep-sea trench, the drowned reef is covered by a blanket of pelagic mud.

(Geologic stages diagram modified from the original classic illustration and concepts of Stearns, 1946, which were upgraded by Macdonald, et al., 1983 and Peterson and Moore, 1987; also incorporated are the many concepts presented in the landmark 2002 publication, Hawaiian Volcanoes: Deep Underwater Perspectives, edited by Takahashi, et al.)

Tectonic Plate Model
Hawaiian-Emperor Volcanic Chain

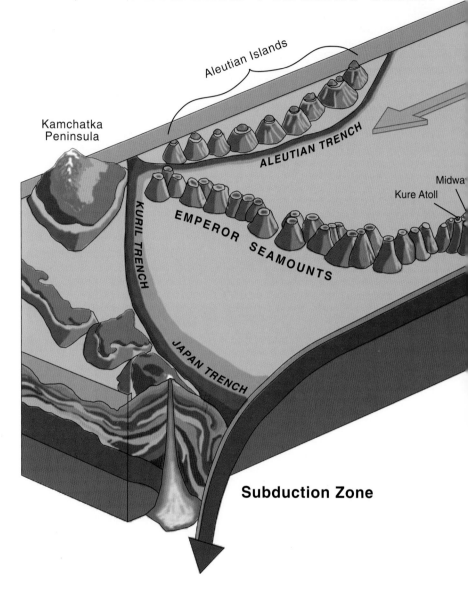

Aleutian Islands

Kamchatka
Peninsula

ALEUTIAN TRENCH

Midwa

Kure Atoll

KURIL TRENCH

EMPEROR SEAMOUNTS

JAPAN TRENCH

Subduction Zone

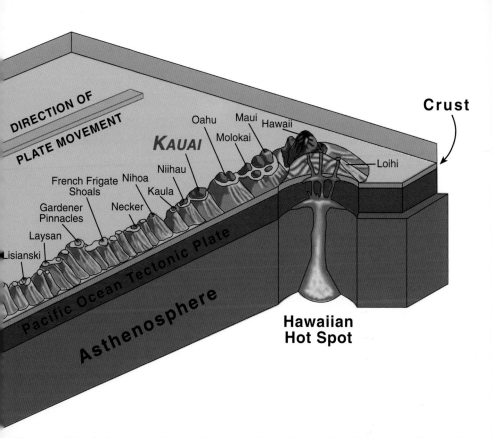

FIGURE 19.   Schematic block diagram of the **Hawaiian-Emperor Volcanic Chain**. The volcanic mountain-islands of Hawaii, and associated seamounts to the northwest, were produced at a **mid-ocean magmatic hot spot** as partial melting of upper mantle material at depths of **35-105 miles** (60-170 km) produced molten magma, which was in turn forced upward through the more rigid oceanic crust. The actual mechanism of magma production is not well understood, but the **10-15% volume increase** associated with the transformation of crystalline rock to molten magma and **buoyancy** of the less dense magma have been the main forces driving the magma upward. As the **Pacific Oceanic Tectonic Plate** has moved across the **Hawaiian Hot Spot** (now located beneath Hawaii Island) a chain of oceanic volcanic mountains, the planet's largest, has been constructed. However, over tens of millions of years those mountains and associated islands have subsided, been degraded by structural failure, and undergone extensive weathering and erosion to produce, successively, low islands, reef shoals/atolls and submerged seamounts. All of that destruction occurred as the chain of mountain-islands continued to move slowly (3-4 inches/year) but steadily toward their total obliteration at the subduction zone boundary with the Asian Continental Tectonic Plate. The **oldest seamounts** of this system are known to have been created at the hot spot **over 70 million years** ago. It is likely that such mountain-island systems existed in a similar way previously for 100's of millions of years.

TECTONIC FEATURES OF THE PACIFIC BASIN

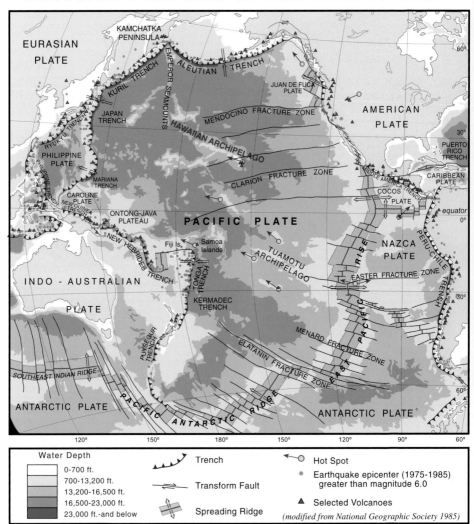

FIGURE 20. Simplified view of the Pacific Ocean Basin displaying major features of the **Pacific Tectonic Plate**. The plate is bounded principally by **oceanic ridges** (Antarctic Ridge and East Pacific Rise) to the south and southeast, and **subduction zone oceanic trenches** to the west and north. As old oceanic plate complexes are subducted below continental tectonic plates at the oceanic trenches, new sea floor is created at the ridges by convectional upwelling of basaltic material from the Earth's mantle. The massive slab of **seafloor spreads** at a rather uniform rate. The Pacific Plate is now moving northwestward at **3 to 4 inches/year**. Mid-ocean volcanic mountain-island chains, such as the Hawaiian Islands and others of Polynesia, are created by eruption of magma from isolated, but relatively stationary, **hot spots** as the tectonic plate moves by. Explosive volcanic activity at the northern and western subduction zones of the Pacific Plate represent much of the famous **"Ring of Fire"** of the Pacific Ocean.

TECTONIC MOVEMENT OF HAWAIIAN ISLANDS

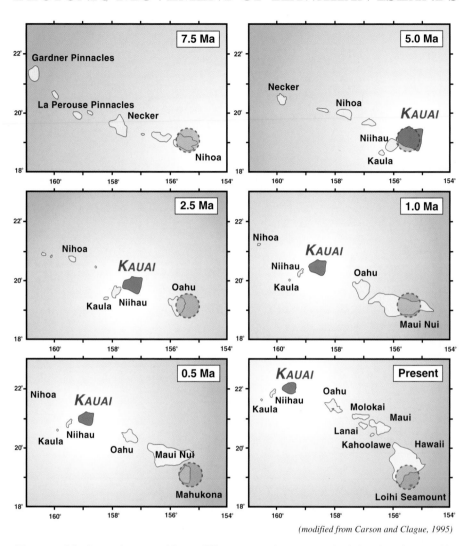

(modified from Carson and Clague, 1995)

FIGURE 21. Over the past 40+ million years the mountain-islands of Hawaii, and the **Pacific Tectonic Plate** upon which they sit, have been moving to the northwest at a rate of about **3.5 inches/year** (8.6 cm/yr). However, the **Hawaiian Magmatic Hot Spot** (red circle), which has been the source of the volcanic-building magma, has remained relatively stationary (being located at latitude 19 degrees North and longitude 155.5 degrees West). This series of maps emphasize the coordinate positions of the **main high volcanic islands of Hawaii** and their **reconstructed positions** at five different times over the past 7.5 million years. The sizes and fused state of islands, ridges and coral reefs (brown) are estimated based on bathymetry and **GLORIA side-scan sonar data.**

TSUNAMI TRAVEL TIMES TO HAWAII

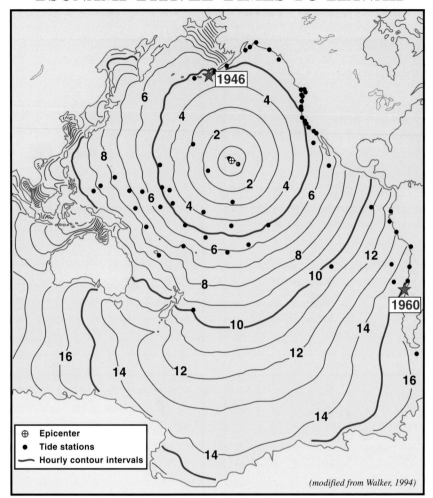

FIGURE 22. Even though Hawaii is in the middle of the North Pacific Ocean, thousands of miles away from active **"Ring of Fire"** edge of the **Pacific Tectonic Plate**, the islands are still susceptible to the devastation of **plate margin earthquakes, landslides and volcanic activity**. Such tectonic events may produce **tsunamis** (Japanese word for "bay wave"). Such waves, commonly referred erroneously in the Unites States as "tidal waves", travel in the open ocean at around **450 to 500 mi/hr**. The **April 1, 1946 tsunami**, originating at Unimak Island, Alaska, struck the Big Island without warning just before 7:00 am; 159 died, 96 in Hilo and 25 (mostly school children) at Laupahoehoe a few miles north of Hilo. The **May 23, 1960 tsunami** originated in Chile, traveled the 6,600 miles to Hawaii in 15 hours and killed 61 people in Hilo even though geologists, Civil Defence officials, and the public knew it was coming. Records are available for numerous other destructive tsunamis that have struck the Hawaiian islands over the past 200 years. Besides the 1946 and 1960 events, Pacific Basin tsunamis of 1837, 1868, 1877, 1923, 1952, 1957 and 1964 left their marks.

TSUNAMI MAGNITUDES IN HAWAII
1900-2002

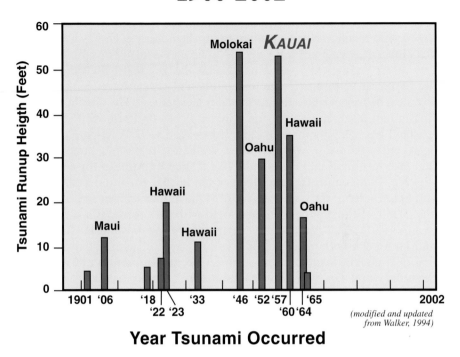

(modified and updated
from Walker, 1994)

Year Tsunami Occurred

FIGURE 23. Tsunamis are **infrequent** and **unpredictable**, just like the tectonic events that generate them. The most destructive tsunamis of the past century in Hawaii have been those of 1946, 1957, 1960 and 1964. The tsunami of 1946, the century's most destructive, struck without warning, like all of those before. Since the early 1950s a sophisticated **tsunami warning system** has been in place in Hawaii. It has had an interesting history of success and failure, but has undoubtedly saved many lives, as it surely will do in the future. **Tsunami magnitude** is indicated in feet of **run up**, referring to the elevation (height above sea level) that a wave will run up on (i.e., flood) the land. As indicated above, 12 sizeable tsunami events occurred in the first 65 years of 20th century; that's **one about every 5 to 6 years**. It makes the past 37+ years seem anomalous. With the continued urban development of low-lying coastal areas around many of the main Hawaii Islands, including Kauai, it is inevitable that **the next sizeable tsunami** will result in great property damage. Hopefully the public will be properly warned and instructed as to evacuation procedures such that loss of life will be minimal.

KAUAI ISLAND
A GEOLOGICALLY MATURE VOLCANIC MOUNTAIN-ISLAND
WITHIN THE "TRADES"

Kauai is a small island. It's only the fourth largest of the main eight high volcanic islands of the Hawaiian Archipelago. However, it is well known as the **oldest at over 5 million years.** Niihau may actually be a bit older, but not by much, geologically speaking. Kauai also is commonly referred to as **"The Separate Kingdom"** due to the relatively great interisland distance (100 miles) between Oahu and Kauai, and is nicknamed **"The Garden Island"** owing in part to having one of the rainiest places on Earth, Mt. Waialeale. The island has aged geologically, but it has aged well. Compared with the "Big Island" of Hawaii, with it's huge, geologically-young, smooth "Baby Huey"-like profile, Kauai looks more like **"The Old Man in the Sea"**, with its lowered, sunken profile and deep, wrinkle-like erosional valleys. The **mature character** of the island is a result of the millions of years of interaction of the island's **lithosphere** (i.e., land area) with the other major elements of the Earth's surface, the **atmosphere, hydrosphere** and **biosphere.** The diverse island landscape is the product of a wide variety of geological processes acting over a significant amount of time. The **phenomenon of Waialeale,** perhaps the world's most perfect **"rain machine"** is a product of the structural development of a cliff that faces the **prevailing trade winds** of the subtropical North Pacific Ocean. These are some of the topics dealt with in the following over-view illustrations.

Kauai has fully progressed into the **"dominantly destructive phase"** of the geologic stages of the Hawaiian volcanic mountain-island system. From a period of about **6 to 5 million years ago** the volcanic mountain built up from nearly **18,000 feet below sea level** to a height as much as **10,000 feet or more above sea level.** The resulting **instability** of such rapid growth, common for all the mid-oceanic shield volcanoes of Hawaii, led to apparent **catastrophic structural failure** to produce features such as the **west scarp of Waimea Canyon** and portions of the **Na Pali Coast.** A probable **second large shield volcano** built the eastern part of the island back only also fail again as it slipped down to create the expansive **Lihue Basin** and the windward-facing scarp of **Mt. Waialeale.** A remnant, western flank, of that postulated volcano persists as the Olokele Plateau, upon which the high, flat island-top bog, the unique **Alakai Swamp,** is developed.

Kauai's mountain-island has **migrated** from its point of origin, near the present location of Hawaii Island, some **350 miles** during the past **6 million years.** Early on it probably rose slightly up over the Hawaiian Bulge, now near Molokai and Oahu, then started its **slow subsidence,** which will continue for the next 25-30 million years until what's left of the island slips below sea level. During an additional 50 million years the submerged volcanic mountain will continue its slow (3-4 inches/year) ride on the **Pacific Tectonic Plate** to finally be reabsorbed into the Earth's mantel in the **subduction zone** near the far northwestern margin of the Pacific Basin.

Over the past 5 million years numerous **geological processes** have been operating on the island. **Intensive weathering** and **erosion** of the relatively unstable volcanic rocks of Kauai has sculpted magnificent valleys, producing lush, life-giving **watersheds.** Huge **waves** coming from all directions in the Pacific Ocean have helped erode the coast and carry away the sedimentary products of the degradation by the atmosphere, hydrosphere and biosphere. At the same time a minor constructive process has been going on. **Biogenic reefs,** comprised mainly of coral and coralline algae, have grown like a "fringe" around the island. The reefs have provided skeletal material for fragmentation, transport and deposition at the shoreline to produce the beautiful alluring **sandy beaches** of the island.

In addition to the **geographic isolation** of the Islands of Hawaii their **location** at the **margins of the tropics** and inside a belt of **persistent trade winds** defines their **essence.** It's an essence highlighted not only by unique isolated-island **biodiversity** but also by refreshing warm, moist winds and amazingly **varied ecosystems** that range from extreme rain forests to deserts within very short distances across and around an island. **Kauai is a compact, closed terrestrial environmental system displaying tremendous internal diversity.** It's the combination of **geology, geographic isolation** and **atmosphere** that has provided for the unique **topography, climatology** and **ecology** of this amazing island.

KAUAI REFERENCE MAP

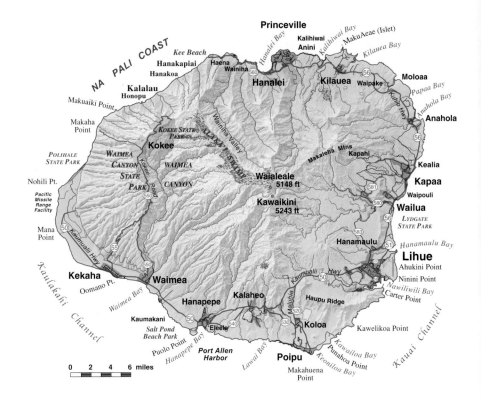

FIGURE 24. Kauai, with a land area of **553.2 square miles,** is the fourth largest of the main high islands of the Hawaiian Archipelago. It's width east-west is about 32 miles and north-south 22 miles. The variable smooth to indented **perimeter is 111 miles.** The highest point is Mt. Kawaikini at 5,243 feet. Lihue is the county seat, with the island's only major airport nearby. Nawiliwili Harbor is the principal harbor. Driving distance from Lihue west to Waimea and Kekaha is 23 and 25 miles, respectively, and north to Princeville and Hanalei 28 and 30 miles, respectively; Kee Beach at the end of the road on the north is 38 miles from Lihue. No road traverses the 14 miles of the Na Pali Coast on the northwest. The residential population (2000 census) is a little over 58,000. Tourism constitutes the main economic base with over one million visitors per year. Principal tourist centers are the Wailua-Kapaa area along the windward coast, Princeville-Hanalei area to the north and Poipu near the southern tip of the island. The Pacific Missile Range Facility (PMRF), operated by the U.S. Navy at Nohili Point (Barking Sands), and agriculture (mainly sugar cane and coffee) are second and third in terms of the island's economic base.

37

KAUAI SPACE PHOTO

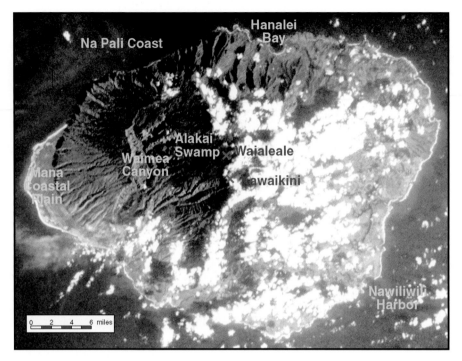

FIGURE 25. Space photo of Kauai Island taken on the 6th flight of the Space Shuttle *Discovery* (August 27 - September 3, 1985). Mt. Kawaikini is the highest point on the island (5,148 ft); however **Mt. Waialeale** (5,148 ft) is better know because of its rain gauge, which has recorded an average **annual rainfall of 430 inches** since 1912. Other physiographic features well displayed in this photo include Waimea Canyon, Alakai Swamp, Mana Coastal Plain and Na Pali Coast. The locations of Nawiliwili Harbor, near the county seat of Lihue, and Hanalei Bay on the north coast also are indicated. The view is of a typical **trade wind day** with clouds present over much of the eastern, windward half of the island and clear skies across the western, leeward half. Such is the situation on Kauai for over **75% of the year**. Central and windward parts experience abundant rainfall and leeward areas are dry. Ecosystems range, within a short distance, from extreme rain forests and swamps to semiarid deserts. Such conditions are a result of two main aspects, **Kauai's Geologic History** and the island's location within the **North Pacific Trade Wind Belt**.

High-Angle Oblique View
of Kauai Island from Southeast

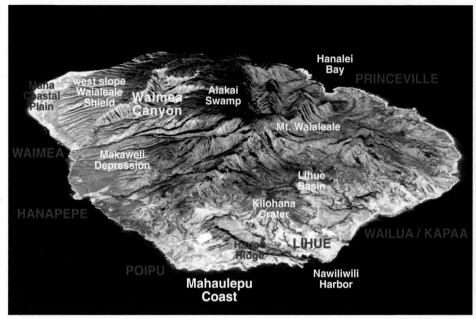

(View produced by Peter Mouginis-Mark, HIGP/SOEST, University of Hawaii under the "Hawaii Synergy" Project, 2003)

FIGURE 26. Computer-generated high-angle oblique view of Kauai from the southeast illustrating **major topographic features** and **patterns of vegetation**. Colors are relatively true based on satellite photos. Carefully selected portions of photos from numerous passes over the island were used to produce this **cloud-free image**. Green patterns dominating the eastern parts of the island are indicative of more **extensively vegetated windward areas** that have received orographic rain. The dark green pattern of the **Alakai Swamp**, situated on the Olokele Plateau, indicates the **dense vegetation** in this very **wet ecosystem**. Yellowish-brown patterns through the west, especially Waimea Canyon and the western slope of Kauai's initial shield volcano, reflect **less vegetative cover** in the **drier leeward areas**. **Waimea Canyon** is well illustrated with fault-generated western scarp and major tributaries that extend eastward to tap the **reddish-brown, botanical-acid-rich water** of the Alakai Swamp. The dry **Mana Coastal Plain** is rimmed by the **state's longest contiguous beach system**, extending for over 16 miles from the Waimea River mouth to the Na Pali Coast. The relatively large rejuvenation-stage lava dome of **Kilohana Crater** covers much of the structural depression of the **Lihue Basin**. **Mt. Waialeale**, one of Earth's rainiest locations, is illustrated in a rare cloud-free state, situated like a giant faucet at the top of the western scarp of the Lihue Basin and the apex of the Alakai Swamp. The **Mahaulepu Coast** area near Poipu lies ready to catch the "island's breath" as trade winds speed up around the high ridges of Haupu at the southeastern corner of the island.

HIGH-ANGLE OBLIQUE VIEW
OF KAUAI ISLAND FROM NORTHWEST

(View produced by Peter Mouginis-Mark, HIGP/SOEST, University of Hawaii under the "Hawaii Synergy" Project, 2003)

FIGURE 27. Computer-generated high-angle oblique view of Kauai from the northwest illustrating **major topographic features** and **patterns of vegetation**. Colors are relatively true based on satellite photos. Carefully selected portions of photos from numerous passes over the island were used to produce this **cloud-free image**. Green patterns dominating the eastern parts of the island are indicative of more **extensively vegetated windward areas** that have received orographic rain. The dark green pattern of the **Alakai Swamp**, situated on the Olokele Plateau, indicates the **dense vegetation** of that **wet ecosystem**. The deep valleys of **Wainiha** and **Lumahai** formed mainly from erosion as a result of the tremendous amount of runoff from the central island area of **Mt. Waialeale** and **Alakai Swamp**. Yellowish-brown patterns throughout the west, especially Waimea Canyon and the western slope of Kauai's initial shield volcano, reflect **less vegetative cover** in the **drier leeward areas**. The dramatic **Na Pali Coast**, which extends for over 14 miles along the northwestern part of the island, displays **1000-2000+ ft sea cliffs** that resulted in part from catastrophic structural failure (i.e., large-scale faulting) early in the development of the main Waialeale Shield around 5 million years ago. Major valleys such as **Hanakapiai, Kalalau, Honopu** and others resulted from headward erosion along the coastal fault scarp. The dry **Mana Coastal Plain** is rimmed by the **state's longest contiguous beach system**, extending for over 16 miles from the Waimea River mouth to the Na Pali Coast.

GEOLOGY OF KAUAI

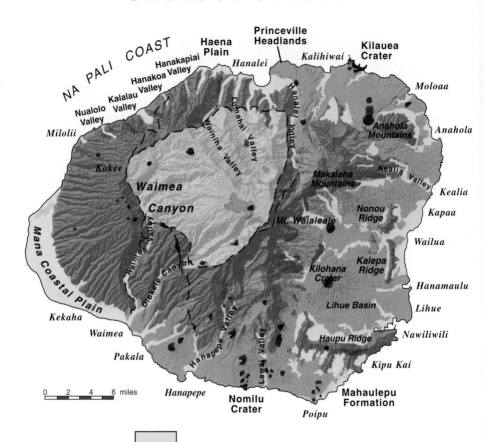

Na Pali Coast
Haena Plain
Princeville Headlands
Kilauea Crater
Hanakapiai
Hanakoa Valley
Kalalau Valley
Nualolo Valley
Milolii
Hanalei
Kalihiwai
Moloaa
Lumahai Valley
Wainiha Valley
Hanalei Valley
Anahola Mountains
Anahola
Kokee
Makaleha Mountains
Kealia Valley
Kealia
Waimea Canyon
Mt. Waialeale
Nonou Ridge
Kapaa
Waimea Valley
Olokele Canyon
Kilohana Crater
Kalepa Ridge
Wailua
Hanamaulu
Mana Coastal Plain
Lihue Basin
Lihue
Kekaha
Hanapepe Valley
Lawai Valley
Haupu Ridge
Nawiliwili
Waimea
Pakala
Kipu Kai
Hanapepe
Nomilu Crater
Mahaulepu Formation
Poipu

0 2 4 6 miles

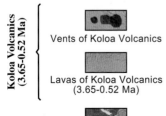
Alluvium; Beach and Dune Sand;
Lagoonal Clays and Marls

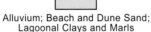
Lithified Calcareous Dune Sand
(4-350 Ka)

Koloa Volcanics (3.65-0.52 Ma)

Vents of Koloa Volcanics

Lavas of Koloa Volcanics
(3.65-0.52 Ma)

Breccia and Conglomerate of
Palikea Formation

– – – – Buried fault scarp

Waimea Canyon Basalt (5.10-3.92 Ma)

Lava of Makaweli Member
(4.16-3.92 Ma)

Lava of Olokele Member
(3.95 Ma)

Lava of Haupu Member
(? 5.10-4.35 Ma)

Lava of Napali Member
(5.10-4.35Ma)

(Modified from Macdonald, Davis and Cox, 1960)

41

FIGURE 28. Geologic map of Kauai. Geologic maps display the distribution, orientation and mutual relationships of major rock types. For a geologist they are absolutely critical displays. This map, published in 1960, is a bit outdated but still displays the main geologic units of Kauai Island. Exposures of the **Napali Member** of the **Waimea Canyon Basalt** (shown in red) have been dated radiometrically at 4.35-5.10 ma (million years); however, those rocks represent only the uppermost portion of the basaltic rocks that formed the primary shield of the volcanic mountain-island. Along the western slopes, west and northwest of Waimea Canyon, the relatively thin-bedded lava flows of the Napali Member dip gently at 8 to 12 degrees away from the center of the island. Similar volcanic rocks comprise the bulk of the mountain to several thousand feet below sea level. Hawaiian volcanoes are built up from the sea floor in as little as 0.5 to 1.0 million years, so the oldest portion of Kauai, at its base some 18,000 feet below sea level, would be only about 6 million years old. The **Olokele Member** (orange) is composed of somewhat thicker, nearly flat-lying lava rock layers dated (one locality only) at 3.95 million years. Previously those layers were interpreted as a caldera-filling sequence. However, today they are thought to represent ponded, basin-filling lava flows that came from a second shield volcano, located in the area of the present Lihue Basin, and ponded up against a fault scarp now represented by the west side of Waimea Canyon. With the Napali Member on the west side and Olokele Member along the east side, **Waimea Canyon displays lava flows on opposite sides with as much as a million years difference in age**. The **Makaweli Member** of the Waimea Canyon Basalt (green), at 4.16-3.92 million years old, fills a down-dropped two-sided fault feature known as the Makaweli Graben. The **Haupu Member** (brown) mapped at the top of Haupu Ridge in the southeastern part of the island is undated; it may be related in origin to the Olokele Member. **Koloa Volcanics** (blue) represent the rejuvenation stage lava flows and explosive vent deposits (black) that erupted mainly at around 2.01-0.52 million years ago. Some Koloa units are significantly older (up to 3.65 million) while other undated units may be considerably younger. Koloa Volcanics cover most of the eastern portion of the island; however, they represent only a thin, veneer-like volcanic layer that comprises less than 1% of the bulk of the mountain-island. Sedimentary deposits of the **Palikea Formation** (purple), which occur between the Waimea Canyon Basalt and Koloa Volcanics, are composed of cliff talus and stream sediments eroded and deposited during the brief break in major volcanic activity between the shield-building and rejuvenations stages of volcano growth. Finally, note the relatively young **sedimentary deposits** (yellow) of the various river valleys and coastal beach/sand dune environments, especially those of the Mana Coastal Plain and Mahaulepu coastal area. Lithified sand dunes of the Mahaulepu Coastal area (now labeled as the **Mahaulepu Formation**) represent cyclic wind-blown sand deposits related to late Pleistocene sea level changes. They may range to as much as 350 thousand years old.

K-Ar Dates on Kauai
(Ages in Millions of Years Ago)

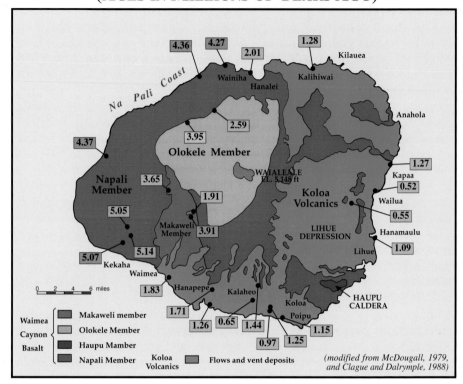

FIGURE 29. Simplified geologic map of Kauai showing the locations of **radiometric age dates** of the island's major volcanic rock units. The absolute ages, in millions of years, were determined using the **potassium/argon** natural radioactive decay system. Lavas of the **Napali Member** of the Waimea Canyon Basalt represent much of the prominent shield-building stage of volcanism, which built the island portion of the volcanic mountain about **5.1-4.3 ma** (million years ago). Lavas of the **Olokele Member** (youngest age 3.95 ma) probably represent western flank flows of a secondary shield volcano once occupying the area of the present Lihue Depression. The **Makaweli Member** (age **4.2-3.9 ma**) filled a north-south trending, graben-like depression. The **Haupu Member** (precise age not known) at the southeastern part of the island is of uncertain origin. Lava flows and explosive volcanic vents of the **Koloa Volcanics** cover most of the eastern half of the island and represent the rejuvenation stage of volcanism which occurred **3.6-0.5 million years ago**. In general the Koloa Volcanics become progressively younger to the east; all flows older than 1.7 m.y. occur in the west-northwest half of the island (e.g. west of Hanapepe Valley and Hanalei Valley) and all flows younger than 1.5 m.y. occur in the east-southeastern half (e.g., east of Hanalei and Hanapepe valleys). The youngest lavas dated (0.52-0.55 ma) occur in the Wailua Valley area.

REJUVENATION STAGE VOLCANIC VENTS

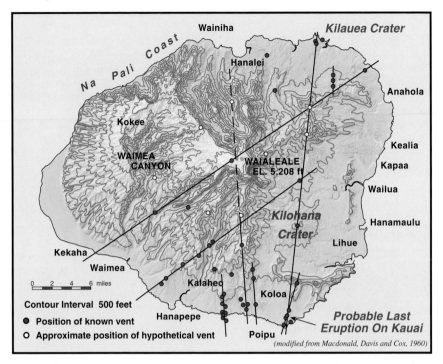

Map legend:
0 2 4 6 miles
Contour Interval 500 feet
● Position of known vent
○ Approximate position of hypothetical vent

Probable Last Eruption On Kauai

(modified from Macdonald, Davis and Cox, 1960)

FIGURE 30. Map of Kauai showing the general location of late, post-erosional, **rejuvenation-stage volcanic vents** of the **Koloa Volcanics**. Most vents (and associated cones) are relatively small volcanic features displaying explosive cinder and spatter deposits; however, some are large. **Kilohana Crater** is a lava dome over 5 miles in diameter and greater than 600 feet high composed mainly of alkalic lava flows that extend eastward across the Lihue Basin but pond up against the western, structural margin of that basin. The composite, cinder/spatter volcanic cone complex at **Kilauea Point** rises up to over 560 feet above the coast at Crater Hill. Some vents apparently exploded through a coastal reef system, as evidenced by large fragments of reef rock within the cinder air-fall deposits that comprise the flanks of what is left of one of the cones. Owing to coastal erosion only about one-third of the Kilauea volcano complex still exists; however, a simple geometric reconstruction indicates that it probably had a diameter of at least 1.2 miles (the famous Diamond Head Crater on Oahu Island would easily fit inside such a cone). The apparent alignment of vents across Kauai suggests the presence of large fissure-like fractures in the shield volcanic dome through which the late-stage lavas and explosive volcanics were emitted. These vents represent the **last volcanic events on Kauai**; however, absolute geologic ages have not yet been determined for any of these features. Most probably erupted **0.5 to 2.0 million years ago**. Some may be considerably younger, but that has yet to be established by absolute geologic dating techniques.

GEOLOGIC STAGES OF KAUAI

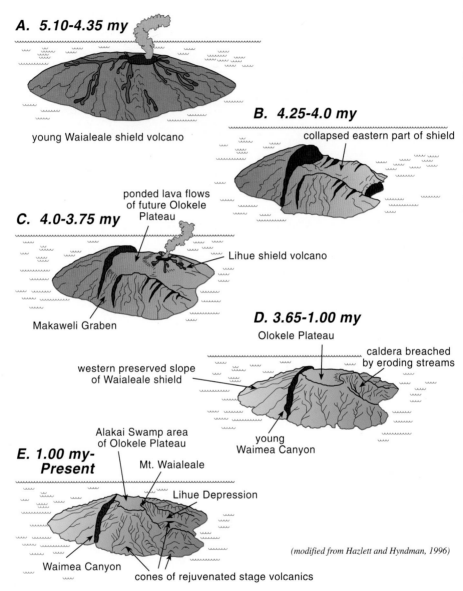

A. 5.10-4.35 my

young Waialeale shield volcano

B. 4.25-4.0 my

collapsed eastern part of shield

ponded lava flows
of future Olokele
Plateau

C. 4.0-3.75 my

Lihue shield volcano

Makaweli Graben

D. 3.65-1.00 my

Olokele Plateau

caldera breached
by eroding streams

western preserved slope
of Waialeale shield

young
Waimea Canyon

Alakai Swamp area
of Olokele Plateau

**E. 1.00 my-
Present**

Mt. Waialeale

Lihue Depression

(modified from Hazlett and Hyndman, 1996)

Waimea Canyon

cones of rejuvenated stage volcanics

FIGURE 31. Schematic of various stages of the geological development of the above sea level portion of Kauai. Emphasized are the origins of major geomorphic features, such as **Waimea Canyon**, the **Olokele Plateau** (upon which the **Alakai Swamp** is developed), and the **Lihue Depression**. Structural development of the fault scarp at the western margin of the Lihue Depression created the precipitous topographic relief that confines orographic lifting of warm, trade wind-driven air to produce so much rainfall at **Mt. Waialeale**.

KAUAI TOPOGRAPHY

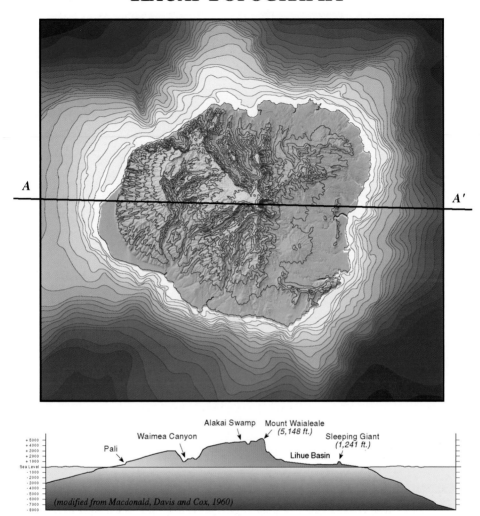

FIGURE 32. Map and topographic profile of the **Kauai shield volcanic dome** illustrating major topographic features. The east-west profile illustrates the **steep eastern scarp of Mt. Waialeale,** which was formed in part by collapse of the Lihue Basin. That precipitous topography creates the dramatic **orographic effect** of the rising and condensation of warm trade wind-driven air and production of the mountain's extreme annual rainfall (> 400 inches). Much of that water drains slowly across the low relief Olokele Plateau resulting in the wet high altitude ecosystem of the **Alakai Swamp. Waimea Canyon** resulted from a complex volcanic-structural history and subsequent weathering and erosion. The **Na Pali scarp** in part represents a significant structural failure of the volcanic dome in which a major northwestern portion of the island slumped down slope.

SEA FLOOR IMAGERY

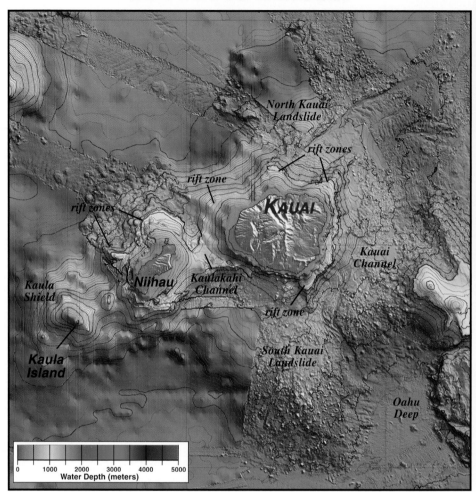

(courtesy of Barry W. Eakins and Joel E. Robinson, U.S. Geological Survey)

FIGURE 33. In recent years oceanographers have implemented their ability to image in great detail the sea floor surrounding the Hawaiian Islands. That has led to a "quantum leap" in our understanding of the geologic origins of the volcanic mountain-island chain. This image of the sea floor surrounding Kauai and Niihau (only a small portion of the data available for the Hawaiian Islands) was derived in part from high-resolution multibeam sonar surveys carried out by the Japan Marine Science and Technology Center (JMSTC) and the University of Hawaii School of Ocean and Earth Science and Technology (SOEST). Of considerable interest are the **gigantic landslide deposits** on the north and south sides of Kauai. Such features probably occurred early in the mountain-island's shield-building stages, 5-6 million years ago when the fast-growing volcano became unstable and failed catastrophically. The point-like projections shaping the submarine perimeter of Kauai's volcanic mountain probably represent **rift-zone extensions**. The Kaulakahi Channel between Kauai and Niihau is only about 850 meters (2550 ft) deep; early on in their history, prior to subsidence, the above sea level portion of **the two islands must have been connected.**

SUBMARINE FEATURES OF KAUAI AND NIIHAU

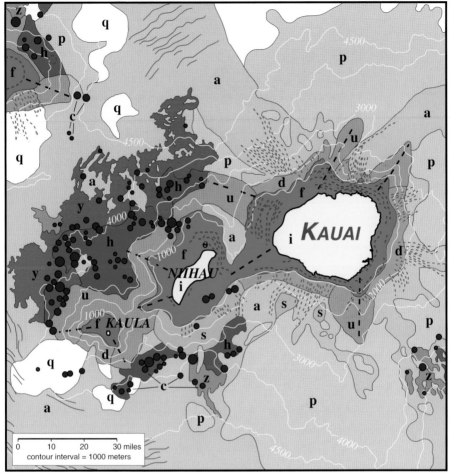

FIGURE 34. The **submarine features** present around the islands of Kauai and Niihau, shown here in this geologic map of the sea floor, are indicative of the **destructive phase** of ocean volcanic mountain-island history. This map was generated principally from GLORIA **side-scan sonar** data. Features indicated include the following: **i**, present island; **f**, area of former island; **a**, smooth apron of island; **d**, steep submarine flank mantled by debris; **s**, slump terrane with fault blocks; **u**, undisturbed lava flows on island flank; **h**, hummocky volcanic terrane; **p**, coarse avalanche deposits; **q**, fine avalanche deposits; **y & z**, mappable lava fields; **c**, small volcanic vent/hill; **radial dashed lines (black)**, rift zones; **concentric lines (red)**; submerged carbonate reef. **Submarine avalanche (i.e., landslide) deposits** probably resulted from **catastrophic structural failure** of the volcanic mountain-island early in its shield-building growth history; for Kauai that was 4-6 million years ago. The "shelf" area between Kauai and Niihau (now the Kaulakahi Channel) is less than 850 meters (2550 ft) deep and probably was emergent early on in the history of the two volcanic mountain-islands 3-5 million years ago.

Kauai Rainfall

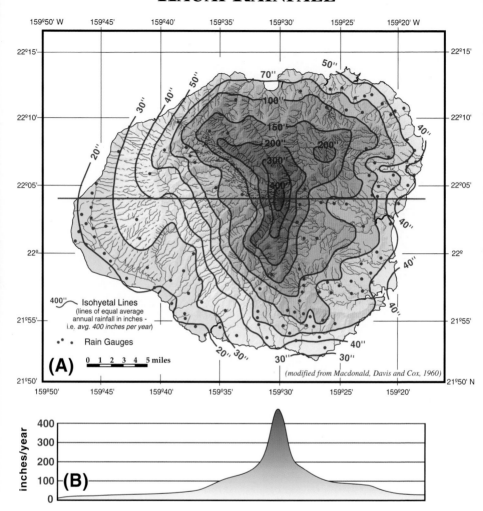

FIGURE 35. Map of Kauai (**A**) showing **drainage patterns** and the general distribution of **annual rainfall** (in inches). **Isohyetal lines** are from the U.S. Weather Bureau. The extreme rainfall near the center of the island at **Mt. Waialeale** results from the **orographic cooling** of warm, moist t**rade wind-driven air** as it is forced up the steep eastern scarp of the mountain. The **cross-plot of rainfall** across the island (**B**) illustrates the **extreme concentration at Waialeale**. Microclimates also are produced in a similar manner in other parts of the island. The result is a relatively compact, isolated, mid-oceanic island with an **extreme diversity of environments**. Ecosystems range from **rain forests** through the windward eastern and central parts of the island to a **high altitude swamp** (the Alakai) and **semiarid desert** settings in the leeward west. Many of the drainages of the dry western part of the island probably were created during past wetter periods, such as times when glaciers covered much of the planet.

AIRFLOW AND OROGRAPHIC LIFTING

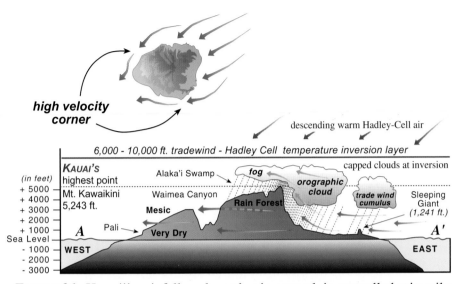

FIGURE 36. Hawaii's rainfall, and weather in general, is controlled primarily by its location within the Earth's **Northeast Trade Wind Belt** and the **topographic relief** of the islands. Rainfall in the **open ocean** around the Hawaiian Islands averages about **25 inches** per year. Overall **average rainfall** for any one of the main high islands is **75-90 inches** per year; however, the distribution of rainfall, and associated ecosystems, across an island displays great **diversity**. Extreme variation in rainfall across most of the main islands in Hawaii is a result of a phenomenon known as **orographic lifting** ("oro" is the Latin word for mountain). As warm, moist, trade wind-driven air rises up on the windward (eastern/northeastern) side of an island the air is cooled. Since cold air can not retain as much moisture as warm air, condensation occurs producing clouds and rain. On **Kauai** air is forced, in a moderately confined manner, nearly straight up the steep eastern scarps of Mts. Waialeale and Kawaikini to dump tremendous volumes of water in their summit areas. For nearly a hundred years the infamous **rain gage at Waialeale** has recorded an average annual rainfall of **430 inches**. Much of that water drains slowly across the Olokele Plateau, creating the high altitude **Alakai Swamp**. Air that reaches the leeward (western) portions of the island is dry, resulting in clear semiarid conditions across areas of Waimea Canyon, the island's mountainous western slope, and the Mana Coastal Plain. A temperature inversion layer (also known as the **trade wind inversion layer**), which is created by descending warm Hadley Cell air, occurs above about 6,000 to 7,000 feet; however, that has little effect on Kauai (maximum elevation of just over 5,000 feet). On Hawaii Island and parts of Maui the above 10,000 ft summits of volcanic mountains such as Mauna Loa, Mauna Kea and Haleakala are clear and dry throughout most of the year owing to a lack of clouds in the somewhat warmer air above the trade wind inversion layer.

GLOBAL ATMOSPHERIC CIRCULATION

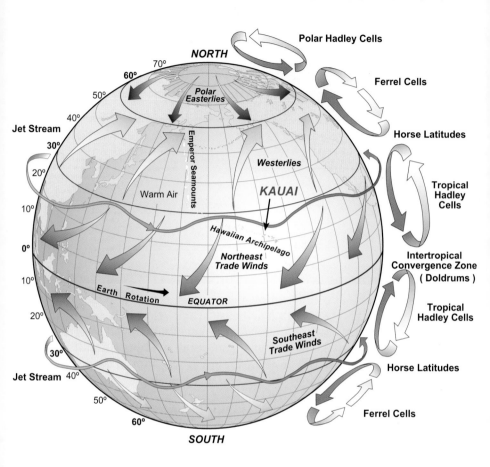

FIGURE 37. Hawaii's exemplary climate, one of the state's most important natural resources, results from its **ideal location** -- related of course to the **archipelago's geologic origin**. The main, inhabited, high islands lie at the margins of the tropics and inside a belt of **persistent trade winds** and accompanying upper-level atmospheric **downwelling**. Such movements of the near-surface atmosphere are a consequence of global circulation. A major component of the atmospheric circulation begins with the rising of air heated near the equator, which drives the **Hadley Cell system** in each hemisphere. The warm air moves poleward at high altitudes, sinks back to the surface at around latitude 30 degrees and then returns to the equator. In the Northern Hemisphere, air moving back to the equator is deflected by Earth's rotation to flow from northeast to southwest. The resultant persistent **Northeast Trade Winds**, in association with the **trade wind inversion** phenomenon and **island topography**, is responsible for Hawaii's most favorable weather and the incredible **climatic diversity** displayed on each of the main high islands.

SEASONAL WIND PATTERNS

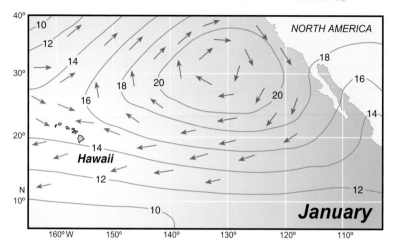

(units of pressure in millibars above 1000 mb)

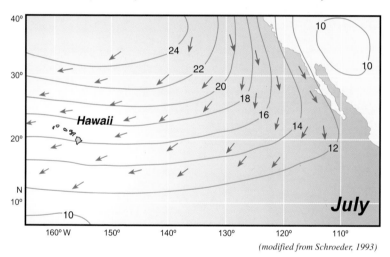

(modified from Schroeder, 1993)

FIGURE. 38. Descending air from the Hadley Cell global atmospheric circulation system interacts with seasonally varying ocean surface temperature to create nearly permanent, quasicircular high-pressure systems known as **subtropical anticyclones**. In the Northern Hemisphere anticyclones produce winds that spiral outward in a clockwise fashion. The trade winds that reach Hawaii originate from the **North Pacific anticyclone**, located northeast of the Islands. **Seasonal shifting** of the location of the North Pacific anticyclone results in noticeable variation in the character of the **Northeast Trade Winds** (red arrows) through the year. In **summer**, with the anticyclone farther north, winds are stronger and more persistent. During **winter**, with the anticyclone farther south, weaker, or sometimes absent, Pacific Ocean storms move closer to the Hawaiian Islands, often disrupting the trade winds and related weather conditions.

MT. WAIALEALE - EASTERN SCARP

FIGURE 39. The **windward-facing eastern "flank" of Mt. Waialeale** may be the world's best **"rain machine"**. This no-rainfall-day view from the upper North Fork of the Wailua River is of **Kauai's most precipitous pali** (Hawaiian for "cliff"). Relief is nearly **3200 feet over a 1/2 mile** horizontal distance from around 2000 feet at the base to 5,148 feet at the summit. Sea cliffs of the island's Na Pali coast display less than 2000 feet of relief. Waimea Canyon ranges up to 2750 feet deep. Wainiha Valley ranges up to 3500 feet deep across a width of 1.5 to 2.0 miles. When in full operation during the **orographic lifting** of warm, moist trade wind-driven air, this gullied, eroded east face of the mountain ranges from a myriad of waterfalls to a sheet of water. The eastern scarp of Waialeale is a **structural scarp** resulting most likely from the **subsidence** (i.e., down-faulting) **of the Lihue Basin** to the east. It does **not** represent the summit or central vent of the Kauai's shield volcano.

MOUNT WAIALEALE RAINFALL
(1912 - 2002)

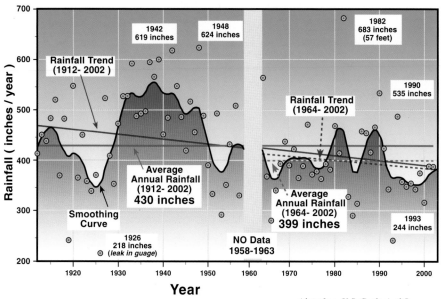

(data from U.S. Geological Survey, Water Resources Division, Lihue, Kauai)

<u>**FIGURE 40.**</u> Since 1912 the measurement of rainfall by a succession of rain gauges installed at the **5,148-foot summit of Mt. Waialeale** has established the mountain as one of the rainiest, if not **the rainiest**, on Earth. Annual rainfall data recorded for 85 years of the 91 year interval of time (no data for the 6 years from 1958-63) has averaged **430 inches** (almost 36 feet). The considerable variation in annual rainfall is a result of a number of factors, in addition to the actual amount of rain falling at the rain gauge location. A leaky tank resulted in a low of 218 inches recorded in 1926. Until the 1960s the Waialeale gauge was read six or more times a year by dedicated meteorologists making an **arduous 3-4 day journey** on horseback and by foot up to and through portions of the Alakai Swamp. Over the years a **number of rain gauges** have been utilized, including a monstrous one installed in 1920 that could measure up to 900 inches of cumulative rainfall. **Since 1963** newer, **state-of-the-art gauges** have been utilized that could be monitored remotely and serviced by helicopter. During the first 19 years of recordings (**1912-30**) annual rainfall averaged **412 inches**. The 20-year period from **1931-1950** averaged a whopping **520 inches**. Since the installation of more sophisticated gauges in 1963 (39 years, **1964-2002**) annual rainfall has averaged **399 inches**. The **last 10 years** (1993-2002) has seen the average drop to **362 inches**. Other places in the world have recorded greater one-year rainfall. For example Cherrapunju, India recorded 905 inches in 1861. However, few places have consistently recorded as much rainfall as Waialeale year after year after year.

THE SKIES OF KAUAI AND NIIHAU

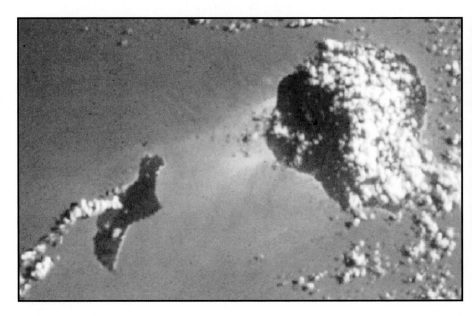

FIGURE 41. Space photo displaying the distribution of clouds over **Kauai** and the neighboring island of **Niihau** during a typical summer day. For scale note that the maximum east-west distance across Kauai is about 32 miles; it's a little over **17 miles across the Kaulakahi Channel** to Niihau which has a maximum north-south dimension of about 22 miles. The extensive cloud cover across the windward (eastern) half of Kauai is a result of the **orographic lifting** and cooling of warm, moist **trade wind-driven air**. During summer months (May-September) such conditions occur as much as 90% of the time. The topography of Kauai, rising up to over 5000 feet at Mts. Waialeale and Kawaikini, forces the condensation of moisture from the air of the **Northeast Trade Winds** to produce hundreds of inches of annual rainfall in the island's central highlands. Moisture depleted air continues its flow across the leeward (western) side of Kauai and on to Niihau. A wide range of environmental systems results from such distribution of moisture. On Kauai **ecosystems** range, within very short distances, from extreme **rain forests** and a **high altitude bog** (Alakai Swamp) to **mesic forests** and **semiarid deserts**. Owing to its low relief (highest elevation of less than 1,300 feet) and its location in the wind shadow of the **"Garden Island" of Kauai**, the **"Forbidden Island" of Niihau** is mostly dry. Even if access wasn't mostly prohibited by private ownership, Niihau, with its lack of abundant water, could never self sustain a large human population.

KAUAI WINDS AND WAVES

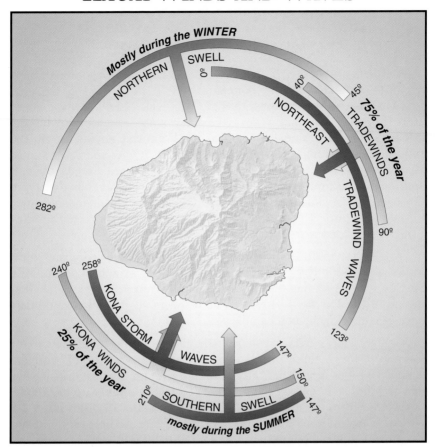

FIGURE 42. Kauai and the rest of Hawaii's main islands experience their own weather created by local atmospheric conditions; however, being in the **middle of the planet's largest ocean** they also feel the effect of weather over a much larger area. Throughout most of the year the **Northeast Trade Winds** dictate not only the island's local weather but also produce short period wind waves and longer period ocean swells that arrive from the northeast and impinge on eastern and northeastern coastal areas. **Kona** (Hawaiian for leeward) **storms** are low-pressure systems that develop in the subtropics at high altitudes and gradually extend toward the ocean surface. During winter months a few Kona systems form west of Hawaii and bring moist, southwesterly winds and rain as well as storm wind waves and swells. Also during the winter large **North Pacific Ocean storms** that never reach Hawaii send large ocean swells to the islands creating some of the world's biggest surf along northern coastal areas. During the summer similar waves generated by winter storms in the Southern Hemisphere travel all the way north across the South Pacific Ocean to strike the island's southern coastal areas. **Southern Swell** waves are much smaller, owing to the distance they have to travel; however, they still generate great waves for summer surfing.

WAIMEA CANYON
REVEALING KAUAI'S GEOLOGIC INTERIOR, BUT THE "GRAND CANYON OF THE PACIFIC"?

The dry western half of Kauai is dominated by 1) a portion of the dip slope of the original volcanic mountain-island's shield volcano, referred to as the **Waimea Shield** or sometimes the Waialeale Shield, 2) the extensive **Mana Coastal Plain** that wraps, like a big wing, around the well-aged, weathered and gullied shield remnant, and 3) **Waimea Canyon**, a north-south trending, 13 mile long, 1500-2500 ft. deep chasm with sparsely vegetated lava rock layers. The canyon's river is fed mainly by three east-side tributaries, **Poomau, Koaie and Waialae** which have cut deep canyons that tap the reddish-brown, botanical acid-rich waters of the island's mountain-top bog, the **Alakai Swamp.** Thus the name: *wai* = fresh water, *mea* = reddish-brown; or, freely translated to *Red River.*

It's easy to understand why many visitors might compare Kauai's famous gorge with the world-renowned canyon of Arizona's portion of the Colorado River. Waimea Canyon is commonly referred to as **"The Grand Canyon of the Pacific".** However, no respectable geologist would do so. Consider the following comparables:

Size: The Grand Canyon, actually only a portion of the canyon of the Colorado River, extends across northwestern Arizona for **277 miles.** It averages **10 miles in width,** from rim to rim, with the greatest distance being about 18 miles and the least about 5 miles. It has a **depth of up to 5700 feet,** as measured from the north rim. Waimea Canyon is **13 miles long, 2-2.5 miles wide** and, if you climb to the very tip of Puu Ke Pele (3/4 mile north of Waimea Canyon Lookout) you will be about **2750 feet** above the river.

Rocks: The prodigious layers of sandstone, shale and limestone that comprise the main **sedimentary rock units** of the Grand Canyon range in age from **as old as 570 to as "young" as 250 million years.** Metamorphic rocks in the deep gorge of the canyon have been estimated to be as old as **1.7 to 2.0 billion years.** The lava rocks of Waimea Canyon range from a little over **5 million** years old to as young as 4 million.

Rock Extent: The same book-like, sedimentary **rock layers** of the Grand Canyon **extend entirely across the canyon,** with the rather flat-appearing, Permian age Kaibab Limestone capping the vast sequence to define the plateau into which the canyon down cut. The west side of Waimea Canyon displays relatively thin lava flow layers of the 5+ million year old Na Pali Member of the Waimea Canyon that dip westward at 8-12 degrees. The east side of the canyon is composed of relatively thick, nearly flat lying lava rock layers of the 3.5-4 million year old Olokele Member of the Waimea Canyon Basalt, i.e., **the rocks on either side of Waimea Canyon differ in age by over 1 million years.**

Formation: The ancestral "Colorado River" of North America has had a complex 60-70 million year long history; however, it did not start eroding what we now call the Grand Canyon until sometime between 5 and 10 million years ago. It down cut as the vast **Colorado Plateau was slowly uplifted.** The Waimea Canyon is a result of a complex **structural, volcanic, and erosional history.** Sometime shortly after the maximum growth of Kauai's **original shield** volcano (most certainly to nearly 10,000 feet above sea level), most of the unstable oceanic mountain structure slumped (faulted down and away) to the east, leaving a precipitous east-facing scarp. A **second shield** volcano, commonly referred to as the "Lihue Shield" built back up the eastern portion of the island about 4 million years ago and shed flows of liquid lava westward to pond against the structural scarp. Subsequently that second volcano subsided (sunk) to form the present Lihue Basin. Since then **weathering** (oxidation and hydration) and **erosion** of the lava layers of both sides by running water widened the canyon as the river cut down mainly along the structural boundary of the different rock units, east and west. The widening and down-cutting of Waimea Canyon has taken place as **the island has subsided** by at least 3,500 feet.

There are more details, but I think you get the point. **Geologically Waimea Canyon and the Grand Canyon don't match up.**

Another bothersome point is the commonly stated "fact" that the term **"Grand Canyon of the Pacific"** was **coined** by the famous American writer, **Mark Twain.** You can be assured here and now that **Twain did not do that.** Mark Twain (of course the pseudonym for Samuel L. Clemens) did spend several months in Hawaii in **1866** (March 18 – July 19) and did write numerous "letters" of his experience, all of which have now been published (e.g., see *Mark Twain's Letters from Hawaii*, edited by A. Grove Day, 1966). And, Twain did make many often quoted remarks about the islands of Hawaii, including the characterization of them as "the loveliest fleet of islands that lies anchored in any ocean". However, **Mark Twain never visited the island of Kauai, never saw Waimea Canyon and most likely never wrote anything about the Grand Canyon of anywhere. Anita Manning** and **DeSoto Brown** of the **Bishop Museum** in Honolulu have researched this topic extensively and have produced an insightful chronology that clears the matter. They point out, among several other things, that 1) the renown geologist John Wesley Powell did not begin his exploration of the entire Colorado River until 1867, 2) in his 1875 publication *Explorations of the Colorado River of the West* Powell does not refer to a "Grand Canyon" and 3) the Grand Canyon was not set aside as a national monument by President Teddy Roosevelt until 1908 (Manning and Brown, personal communication, October 2003). Again note that Twain was in Hawaii in 1866. He did come into Honolulu Harbor in 1895 on a world tour, but did not disembark owing to a cholera epidemic in the then Republic of Hawaii [numerous events were planned but were cancelled when he couldn't get off the ship]. **Mark Twain died in 1910.**

It's not known exactly when the Waimea Canyon was first "formally" referred to as the "Grand Canyon of the Pacific", but most likely it was in something written in the mid-1900s to attract visitors to Kauai. In a July 3, **1917 article in Kauai's Garden Island newspaper** (*National Park for Kauai*) it is reported that Waimea Canyon was being examined (by a special agent of the federal park commission) for consideration as a national park. At the time there were only 17 national parks. There is no mention of a grand canyon in the article. An April 12, **1921** article (*Growing Popularity of Puu-ka-Pele Park*) there is mention of a Mr. F. Grinnell (of the High School on Kauai) taking a Dr. J.C. Hoag of Chicago on a horseback tour of the Puu-ka-Pele-Kokee region. Dr. Hoag was very much impressed and compared Waimea Canyon with the Grand Canyon of Colorado, with which he was familiar. In a February 16, **1926** Garden Island article titled *Waimea Canyon Not To Be a National Park – Cammerer Agrees better Suited to Be Under the Control of the Local Authorities* there still was no mention of a grand canyon. So if anyone might get credit for the concept "Grand Canyon of the Pacific" perhaps it should be **J.C. Hoag.**

Waimea Canyon - East Side
(View from Waimea Canyon Lookout)

Alakai Swamp

Poomau Canyon

Koale Canyon

<u>Figure 43</u>. The **Waimea Canyon Lookout**, located near mile marker 10 along **State Highway 550,** is one of the island's most visited places. Here the canyon is **2-2.5 miles wide** and over **2500 feet deep** (elevation of **3320 ft** at lookout to river below with elevation of **800 ft** above sea level). The spectacular east-facing view, the center portion of which is shown here, is dominated by the ridges and valleys of the canyon's east side. **Koaie Canyon** (center) contains Waimea River's largest tributary, extending for nearly 7 miles to it's head waters in the **Alakai Swamp**. A portion of **Poomau Canyon** (approximately 4 miles long) visible at the left also heads in the Alakai. Along with **Waialae Canyon** (to the right but not illustrated above) with its 5-6 mile-long stream, the three tributaries drain **reddish-brown, botanical acid-rich water** off the Alakai Swamp and dump it into the 13 mile long, north-south trending main trunk of the Waimea River. It's that water that gives the river it's name; **wai = "fresh water", mea = "reddish-brown"**. The nearly flat-lying, relatively thick lava flows of the **Olokele Member** of the Waimea Canyon Basalt dominate the east side of the canyon and form the **Olokele Plateau**, upon which the Alakai Swamp is developed. The 4 million year old flows apparently were derived from a now subsided shield volcano that sunk to form the Lihue Basin of eastern Kauai. Those flows contrast significantly with the 5+ million year old, relatively thin and westward sloping flows of the **Na Pali Member** of the Waimea Canyon Basalt (not shown above) that form the western side of the canyon. The **intense weathering** (oxidation and hydration) and **erosion** of the lava flows produces the ledgy, step-wise topography and rust-colored (**iron-oxide**) hues. Relative **lack of vegetation** on this **dry side** of Kauai allows for this view of the colorful rocks and soils.

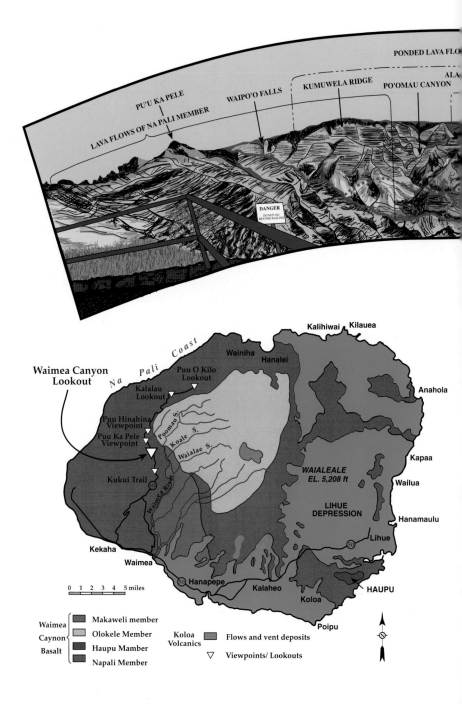

PONDED LAVA FLO

ALA
PO'OMAU CANYON

KUMUWELA RIDGE

WAIPO'O FALLS

PU'U KA PELE

LAVA FLOWS OF NA PALI MEMBER

DANGER
DO NOT GO
BEYOND RAILING

Kalihiwai · Kilauea

Coast

Waainiha

Hanalei

Na Pali

Puu O Kilo
Lookout

**Waimea Canyon
Lookout**

Kalalau
Lookout

Anahola

Puu Hinahina
Viewpoint

Poomau S.

Puu Ka Pele
Viewpoint

Koale S.

Kapaa

*WAIALEALE
EL. 5,208 ft*

Waialae S.

Wailua

Kukui Trail

Waimea River

LIHUE
DEPRESSION

Hanamaulu

Kekaha

Lihue

Waimea

0 1 2 3 4 5 miles

HAUPU

Hanapepe

Kalaheo

Koloa

Poipu

Waimea Caynon Basalt	Makaweli member
	Olokele Member
	Haupu Mamber
	Napali Member

Koloa Volcanics — Flows and vent deposits

▽ Viewpoints/ Lookouts

61

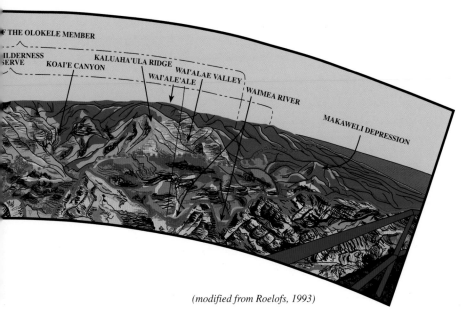

(modified from Roelofs, 1993)

•₊₊₊•• BOUNDARY OF MAKAWELI DEPRESSION ACROSS THE CANYON

∼ INDICATES LIMIT OF SHIELD BUILDING FLOWS ALONG WEST SIDE OF CANYON

<u>FIGURE 44</u>. Panoramic east-facing view from the **Waimea Canyon Lookout** located along **State Hwy 550** leading up to **Koke'e State Park** (see simplified geologic map at left showing principal stops along the highway). Shield-building lava flows of the **Napali Member** of the Waimea Canyon Basalt (age **5.1-4.35 million years**) are visible to the left and dip 8-12 degrees west-northwest away from the center of the principal volcanic shield that comprises the island of Kauai. The relatively thick, flat-lying lava flows of the **Olokele Member** of the Waimea Canyon Basalt (youngest age of **3.95 million years**) are visible to the east across much of the panoramic view. Olokele flows probably originated from a shield volcanic vent located in the eastern portion of the island, flowed westward and ponded up against the western scarp of Waimea Canyon. The Olokele Plateau supports the **Alakai Swamp**, Hawaii's highest bog ecosystem, where much of the water generated by **Mt. Waialeale** drains slowly across the low relief surface. The reddish-brown, botanical acid-rich bog water feeds into tributaries of the Waimea River (mainly those of Koaie, Waialae and Poomau Canyons), giving the river its name; **"waimea" translates as "red river"**. Lavas of the **Makaweli Member** of the Waimea Canyon Basalt (age **4.16-3.92 million years**) are present to the south (lower right portion of view) where they fill a down-dropped, structural depression.

WAIMEA CANYON CROSS-SECTION
(AT WAIMEA CANYON LOOKOUT)

West   East

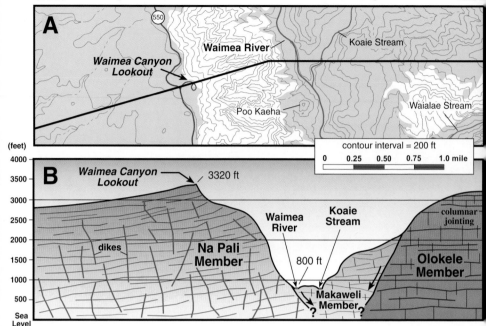

FIGURE 45. One of the truly amazing aspects of Kauai's Waimea Canyon is the **difference in character and age** of the geologic formations that form the sides of the canyon. The **topographic** and **geologic cross-section** shown here (**B**) illustrates the situation. The east-west cross-section (location shown in topographic slice map **A** above) extends through the **Waimea Canyon Lookout** (elevation 3320 ft), across the **Waimea River** (elevation 800 ft) and on to the **Olokele Plateau**, which forms the eastern side of the canyon. Lava flows exposed along the west side of the canyon have been delineated and mapped as the **Na Pali Member** of the Waimea Canyon Basalt. They are characterized as relatively thin lava flow layers (only a few feet thick, or less) dipping (inclined downward) to the west at 8-12 degrees; they display numerous near-vertical lava dikes, which formed from the injection of molten lava into fractures. At greater than **5 million years old**, these flows represent the **original shield volcano** of Kauai. **Structural failure** of Kauai's volcanic mountain-island complex early in its shield-building history resulted in the down-faulting of its eastern portion and creation of the steep west wall of the canyon. Lava flow layers of the **Olokele Member** of the Waimea Canyon Basalt (about **4 million years old**) form the east side of the canyon. They represent lava flows from a second, younger shield volcano that **ponded** up against the western scarp of the canyon, resulting in relatively thick (to tens of feet), flat-lying lava rock layers. Irregular lava flow layers of the **Makaweli Member** of the Waimea Canyon Basalt subsequently filled another local down-dropped structural feature known as the Makaweli Graben. **Weathering** and **erosion** over the past 4 million years has continued to widen and deepen the canyon.

WAIMEA CANYON LAVA FLOWS
(VIEW FROM POOMAU CANYON)

FIGURE 46. Waimea Canyon and its tributaries have cut deep into the shields of Kauai's volcanic mountain-island to provide us a look at its interior. This view westward down the axis of **Poomau Canyon** displays over 1500 feet of the **Olokele Member** of the Waimea Canyon Basalt. The west side of Waimea Canyon is barely visible in the far distance. Although the overall age of the rock formation shown here is on the order of 4 million years, the tens to hundreds of individual **lava flows** each probably represents an eruptive event of only hours to days in duration. Intervals of time between each lava flow may range from hours to years, or even tens to hundreds of years. The total amount of time represented by the 1500-ft thick complex of lava flows displayed here is only **20 to 40 thousand years**. Volcanoes tend to grow up fast and age slowly. The **lack of explosive volcanic deposits**, such as cinder and ash layers, is evidence of the **effusive** (i.e., non-explosive) pouring out of hot liquid magma during the eruption of Hawaii's mid-oceanic shield volcanoes. In general effusive type eruptions are related to the relatively **low silica** and **low water** content of the magma, much of which originates in the Earth's upper mantle. Once lava reaches the surface of the earth, especially the above sea level portion, it encounters **a very caustic environment** we call the **"atmo-sphere"**. Oxygen and water "attack" the rock through chemical reactions such as **oxidation** and **hydration**, which degrade (e.g., soften) it and make it easily susceptible to erosion by running water. Owing to their chemical instability, the lava rocks of Hawaii are some of the **most intensely weathered** (i.e., rotten and unstable) rocks on the planet. There's very good reason why rock climbing is not a popular sporting activity on Kauai.

MAHAULEPU COAST
EXPANSIVE GEOLOGIC HISTORY AND NATURAL BEAUTY

The **southeastern coastline** of Kauai from **Makahuena Point,** the island's southernmost point, to **Kawelikoa Point** lies within the Hawaiian land divisions (ahupuaa) of both Paa and Mahaulepu; however, the area is mostly referred to as the **Mahaulepu Coast.** The straight-line distance between the two prominent points is just a little less than 4.5 miles. Walking distance along the moderately irregular coastline is a little over 5 miles, the first 4 miles of which to Haula Bay is an easy nature walk. The general **NE-SW trending coast** is nearly parallel to the average direction that the **trade winds** blow throughout the year. One might say that this is where **Kauai "takes its breath".** But first, and foremost, this area of Kauai contains/displays/represents the **most extensive, and best-documented history** of anywhere in the main (8 of them) high volcanic islands of the Hawaiian Archipelago.

Rock units of Mahaulepu display the longest and most complete record of geologic time of any one location on the island. Geologic history is represented by 1) remnants of the oldest volcanic rocks of Kauai, including the **5+ million year old Na Pali Member** of the Waimea Canyon Basalt which comprises the base of Haupu Ridge, 2) late, rejuvenation stage volcanic rocks (lava flows, cinder and spatter cones) of the **Koloa Volcanics** (estimated at **0.25 to 1.5 million years old**), and 3) limestones of the **Mahaulepu Formation** representing cycles of coastal sand dunes and reddish soil layers that record the history of sea level change over at least the **past 350,000 years.** Modern calcareous (lime) **beach sediments** and trade wind transported **dune sands** continue to accumulate today as they have during many past sea level high-stands.

In addition to the main geologic rock units of Mahaulepu **more "recent" history** has been recorded in a number of ways. Although such recent history is not dealt with here, it is worth pointing out a few items to emphasize **the expanse of Mahaulepu's record.** Sediments that have been accumulating in the **Makauwahi Sinkhole** (developed by dissolution of the oldest limestone unit of the Mahaulepu Formation) provide a detailed paleontological record of the **past 9,500 years,** including the dramatic impact of human inhabitants beginning about 800-1000 ago (Burney, et al., 2001, Burney and Burney, 2003). **Archaeologic history** of the **past few hundred years** is represented by numerous features, including heiaus (Hawaiian religious/ceremonial structures), rock walls, rock platforms, sand dune burial sites, etc. **Contemporary history** (encompassing Hawaiian oral history) includes accounts of a great battle where war canoes from the other islands of Hawaii **ma-ha`ule-pu**(ed) (i.e., met and **"fell together"**) in an attempt to conquer and bring Kauai into a broader Hawaiian Kingdom. They failed. Also there is the account of Captain James Cook's first journey along the coast just prior to anchoring off the leeward coast of Waimea and landing on Kauai in January 1778. In more recent "recorded" history, the area provides a rich account of sugar cane, whaling ships and a cultural melting pot of local and mostly Asian laborers.

A day spent exploring Mahaulepu is a day of discovering history.

Mahaulepu View

Haupu

Kawelikoa Pt.

Papamoi Sand Dunes

(Twc)

(Qm-Paoo Mbr)

Paoo Pt.

Kawailoa Bay

Kawailoa Beach

Kamala Sand Dunes

FIGURE 47. Panoramic view eastward of the northeastern portion of Mahaulepu. Viewers can experience not only the magnificent beauty of this yet undeveloped coastal area of Kauai, but perhaps can imagine some of the changes that have occurred over a **vast amount of geologic time**. Light-colored, lime beach and dune sediments are accumulating today from the abrasion, transport and deposition of **marine plant** (e.g., algal) and **animal** (e.g., coral) **skeletal material**, much of which is derived from shallow nearshore reefs. The modern Kamala Sand Dunes, shown here moderately stabilized by beach vegetation, have grown as the **trade winds have blown fine- to medium-grained lime sand southwestward** from the adjacent Kawailoa Beach. The dense growth of Australian pine across the bay marks the location of another pile of modern windblown sand (the Papamoi Sand Dunes) which also accumulated from sand blown off a small upwind beach. **Limestones** (ancient lithified sand dunes) of the Paoo Member of the Mahaulepu Formation (Qm) form the low ledge along the northern margin of Kawailoa Bay. That limestone, like the other members of the Mahaulepu Formation, have **lithitified** (i.e., changed from lime sediment into limestone) by a process of **calcite cementation** over tens to hundreds of thousands of years. Like the modern Kamala and Papamoi dunes, the ancient lithified sand dunes of the Mahaulepu Formation accumulated during **high, interglacial, sea level stands** as strong prevailing trade winds blew sand from upwind beaches. Haupu Ridge in the distance is composed of some of the **oldest rocks on the island**. Lava flows of the Napali Member of the Waimea Canyon Basalt (Twc) can be seen dipping gently (7-12 degrees) seaward toward Kawelikoa Point. These volcanic rocks, dated at over **5 million years** old, represent the shield-building stage of Kauai's mountain-island complex. **Geologic processes** operating from the time of the accumulation of lava flows that now form Haupu to the accumulation of ancient sand dunes of the Mahaulepu Formation and modern beach and dune sediment of the Mahaulepu coast have created not only the land forms of this beautiful coastal region, but have sculpted the entire island of Kauai.

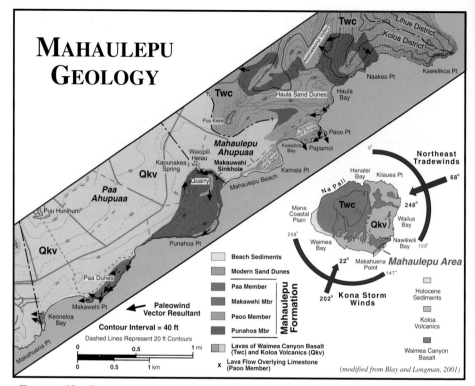

FIGURE 48. Geologic map of the southeast coastal area of Kauai from Makahuena Point (island's southernmost point) to Kawelikoa Point. Coastal zones of the ahupuaas (ancient Hawaiian land divisions) of both Mahaulepu and Paa are present; however, the area is generally known as Mahaulepu. **Rock units** of this area display the **longest and most complete record of geologic time** of any one location on the island. Lavas of the **Waimea Canyon Basalt** (Twc) range in age to greater than 5 million years and represent the shield building stage of Kauai's mountainisland complex. Volcanic vents and lava flows of the **Koloa Volcanics** (Qkv), which represent the rejuvenation-stage of volcanism, range in this area from about 1.5 to less than 0.5 million years old. Limestones of the **Mahaulepu Formation**, which has been divided into the four mappable members shown, represent **cyclic deposition** of **coastal sand dunes** and **soils** in response to **sea level change**. Sea level fluctuations as much as 400 feet were in response to **global glaciation**. During interglacial sea level highs (such as today) trade winds blew beach sediment southwestward along the coast to accumulate as large sand dunes. When sea level was low (during glacial periods) and the shore line was a mile or more offshore, reddish soils covered the inland dunes. Based on knowledge of **global glacial cycles** it has been estimated that the oldest of the limestone members (Punahoa Mbr) accumulated over 300,000 years ago. The youngest member (Paa Mbr) has been dated at 4,000-6,000 years old. Modern sand dunes and beach sediments are again forming in a manner similar to that of the ancient sands. Determinations of **paleowinds** (i.e., ancient winds), based on the study of layering in the lithified sand dunes of the Mahaulepu Formation, indicate that trade wind patterns of past interglacial times were similar to those of today.

GENERAL GEOLOGIC SECTION
MAHAULEPU AREA

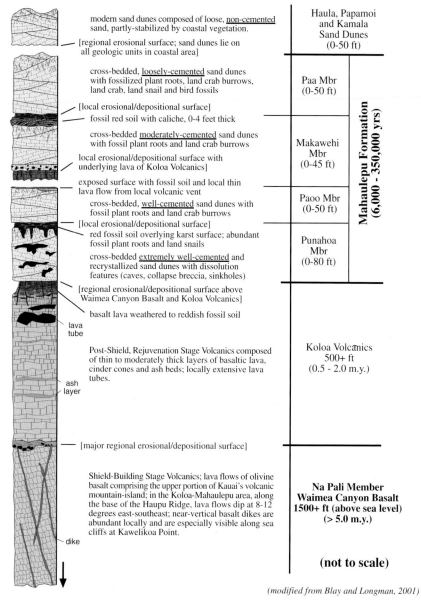

modern sand dunes composed of loose, non-cemented sand, partly-stabilized by coastal vegetation.

[regional erosional surface; sand dunes lie on all geologic units in coastal area]

Haula, Papamoi and Kamala Sand Dunes (0-50 ft)

cross-bedded, loosely-cemented sand dunes with fossilized plant roots, land crab burrows, land crab, land snail and bird fossils

Paa Mbr (0-50 ft)

[local erosional/depositional surface]

fossil red soil with caliche, 0-4 feet thick

cross-bedded moderately-cemented sand dunes with fossil plant roots and land crab burrows

local erosional/depositional surface with underlying lava of Koloa Volcanics]

Makawehi Mbr (0-45 ft)

exposed surface with fossil soil and local thin lava flow from local volcanic vent

cross-bedded, well-cemented sand dunes with fossil plant roots and land crab burrows

[local erosional/depositional surface]

Paoo Mbr (0-50 ft)

red fossil soil overlying karst surface; abundant fossil plant roots and land snails

cross-bedded extremely well-cemented and recrystallized sand dunes with dissolution features (caves, collapse breccia, sinkholes)

Punahoa Mbr (0-80 ft)

[regional erosional/depositional surface above Waimea Canyon Basalt and Koloa Volcanics]

basalt lava weathered to reddish fossil soil

lava tube

Post-Shield, Rejuvenation Stage Volcanics composed of thin to moderately thick layers of basaltic lava, cinder cones and ash beds; locally extensive lava tubes.

ash layer

Koloa Volcanics 500+ ft (0.5 - 2.0 m.y.)

Mahaulepu Formation (6,000 - 350,000 yrs)

[major regional erosional/depositional surface]

Shield-Building Stage Volcanics; lava flows of olivine basalt comprising the upper portion of Kauai's volcanic mountain-island; in the Koloa-Mahaulepu area, along the base of the Haupu Ridge, lava flows dip at 8-12 degrees east-southeast; near-vertical basalt dikes are abundant locally and are especially visible along sea cliffs at Kawelikoa Point.

dike

Na Pali Member Waimea Canyon Basalt 1500+ ft (above sea level) (> 5.0 m.y.)

(not to scale)

(modified from Blay and Longman, 2001)

FIGURE 49. Simplified geologic section of the Mahaulepu area, southeastern Kauai. Rock units of the area display the **longest and most complete record of geologic time** of any one location on the island. Limestones of the Mahaulepu Formation represent **cyclic deposition of lime sand dunes and reddish soils** during **interglacial sea level high stands** and **glacial sea level low stands**, respectively.

LITHIFIED SAND DUNES OF MAHAULEPU

FIGURE 50. Limestones of the Mahaulepu Formation are characterized mainly by the presence of **large-scale cross-bedding**, such as that illustrated here in the Makawehi Member near Makawehi Point and Keoneloa ("Shipwrecks") Beach. Groups of layers of sandstone up to over ten feet thick are **inclined at angles approaching 35 degrees**. Such layering of fine-to medium-grained lime sand is representative of that formed at the front of medium- to large-scale **coastal sand dunes**. The lime sand forming the ancient lithified dunes of Mahaulepu was derived from the abrasion, transport and deposition of **marine skeletal material** such as that of calcareous (i.e., stony) algae, coral and shells (e.g., clams and snails). Sand accumulated initially on the **beaches** by marine wave and current processes. Subsequently the fine-grained fraction of the beach sediment was blown southwestward by the strong prevailing **trade winds** to accumulate as coastal **sand dunes**. All of that happens during **high stands of sea level** that occur during **global interglacial times**. The lithified sand dunes of the Makawehi Member shown here accumulated during the last major interglacial high-stand (before the present one) about 125,000 years ago. The **lithification process**, which converts lime sand into limestone, is one of **cementation**. Some skeletal grains, such as those from coral animals, are composed of relatively **unstable lime minerals** (e.g., aragonite) and **dissolve** in the fresh water that comes from rain and ground water. The dissolved lime material then reforms (**precipitates**) as minute **crystals of calcite** (a more stable lime mineral) that grow on grains and **interlock** with crystals growing on adjacent grains, binding them together. Initial, **weak cementation** can occur within **tens to hundreds of years**. **Harder limestones** are cemented over **hundreds of thousands of years**.

Na Pali Coast
World Class Scenic Geology;
Waves, Structural Collapse, or Both?

Along the northwest and west coasts of Kauai dramatic cliffs dominate the scenery. Na Pali (Hawaiian for *The Cliffs*) extends for 14 miles along the coast from the end of the road at Kee Beach to Polihale Beach. Precipitous sea cliffs range up to 1400 feet high. Other coastal portions display a step like gain in elevation to heights as much as **4000 feet** within only a half a mile from the coast. From Polihale Beach **inland cliffs**, bounded on their seaward margin by the Mana Coastal Plain, then extend southeastward in an arcuate, wrap around manner, for another 12 miles to the Waimea River where they are only 200-400 feet high. In total this cliff topography extends for almost **a quarter of the distance around the island; it's a major feature.** The sea coast portion of Na Pali provides world class scenery and opportunities for outdoor hiking, camping and boating adventures that people come from all over the world to experience. The major valleys along Na Pali were occupied for over a thousand years by hundreds to thousands of pre-European-discovery occupants. The 10 mile trail from Kalalau Valley to Kee Beach was established to provide reasonable access, especially during winter months when the coast is pounded by waves that reach heights of 25-30 feet. Such waves made ocean access to the various valleys impossible, even for the experienced Hawaiian ocean men.

Geologically, Na Pali forms the seaward margin of the **original shield** of Kauai's volcanic mountain-island. It is composed entirely of lava flows of the 5+ million-year-old **Na Pali Member** of the Waimea Canyon Basalt that dip gently (8-12 degrees) coastward in a radial pattern away from the center of the island. Near vertical **lava rock dikes,** which represent fractures injected with molten lava, are common throughout the Na Pali Member; they are visible all along the coast. Weathering and erosion has enhanced definition of the hundreds of lava flows and dikes. Wave undercut **sea caves** are present all along the base of the cliffs. Several major **valleys,** including the two largest – Kalalau and Hanakapiai, have been incised by stream erosion. The amount of **annual rainfall** changes significantly along the coast from over 70 inches at Kee Beach to around 40 inches at Kalalau to less than 20 inches along Polihale Beach and the Mana Coastal Plain.

In map view Na Pali displays considerable variation in shape from one end to the other. From Kee Beach to Makuaiki Point, a distance of 9 miles, the shoreline has a distinct arcuate, **concave seaward shape,** like a big scoop. The largest valleys have been cut by stream erosion into the cliffs along this portion of the coast; the steep headwall of Kalalau Valley at 4000 feet high is over 2.5 miles inland. Vegetation is lush in the Kee Beach area to moderately sparse in the area beyond Kalalau Valley. Continuing on from Makuaiki Point to Polihale Beach and then on around to Waimea, a distance of 14 miles, the coastline is **bowed in the opposite direction,** like a big bulge. The cliffs diminish from

1400 feet high at Makana Point to less than 200 feet at Waimea. Vegetation is sparse in the semi-arid setting around this leeward side of the island.

Thoughts about Na Pali's geologic origin have provided for an interesting **"geocontroversy"**. In 1960 Macdonald, Davis and Cox, who published the most recent geologic map of Kauai, wrote the following:

> "Napali fault. – Dana (1849), and later Powers (1917) and Hinds (1930), considered the cliffs of the Napali Coast to be the result of **wave erosion** of a high northwest-facing **fault scarp**. Stearns (1946) considered them to be wholly the result of wave erosion and rejected the hypothesis of an offshore fault. It is difficult to rule out the possibility of a tangential fault of small displacement, but certainly there is **no necessity of a fault** to explain the existence of the cliffs. **Wave erosion is totally adequate cause**. ... If the Napali fault exists at all, it cannot have any large displacement." (Macdonald, Davis and Cox, 1960, p. 89)

In the late 1980's the U.S. Geological Survey mapped in detail the sea floor surrounding the Hawaiian Islands out to the 200 kilometer limit of the Exclusive Economic Zone and discovered a plethora of **giant submarine landslides** (see Moore, and others, 1989; Moore, Normark and Holcomb, 1994). At least 70 probable landslides were discovered with lengths of over 12.5 miles and some extended for as much as **125 miles.** The presence of these apparent landslides, the planet's largest, was used to explain **the sea cliffs** around the Hawaiian Islands as merely the head walls of giant slump-like **faults,** with **displacements of thousands of feet.** Faulting would have occurred as **catastrophic structural failures.** It has been postulated that such structural failure has been the result of the rapid growth, and resulting structural instability, of the large shields of Hawaii's volcanoes. These are the biggest and fastest growing mountains in the world. **A case of getting too big too fast(?).**

The **problem** is that one theory (wave erosion or faulting) doesn't seem to adequately explain all the features. The scoop like shape of the coast between Kee and Makuaiki Point certainly looks like it could be the headward portion of a giant slump, and it could match up with a broad offshore submarine canyon complex and the North Kauai Submarine Landslide (Figure 33). However, the bulge-like, convex shaped portion of Na Pali from Makuaiki Point around to Polihale and on to Waimea has the shape of a coast eroded by refracting (i.e., wrap around) waves; plus there are no major submarine landslides seaward of this portion of the island. To resolve the issue of the origin of Kauai's Na Pali coast, and other features of Kauai and Niihau, **close-in surveys** of the surrounding seafloor were conducted in **late 2003** by the University of Hawaii's Research Vessel *Kilo Moana*. The senior author of this book was fortunate to be an observer on that cruise. Preliminary results of the survey indicated that **features of the seafloor near offshore of Na Pali and the Mana Coastal Plain** have resulted from **wave erosion and sedimentation,** <u>not</u> from **faulting and landslide emplacement** (Brian Taylor, SOEST, personal communication, December 2003). **The geocontroversy continues**.

NA PALI COAST
(VIEW FROM KALALAU TRAIL)

Hanakapiai Valley

Makuaiki Point

FIGURE 51. The coast line of **Na Pali** (Hawaiian for *The Cliffs*) provides some of Kauai's most spectacular scenery. The precipitous sea cliffs dominate the northwest shore for **14 miles** from Kee Beach at the end of the highway on the north side of the island to Polihale Beach on the west. It is accessible mainly on foot or by boat; no roads. This hiker's eye view southwestward down the coast is from about a mile in on the **Kalalau Trail**, which continues on to **Kalalau Valley**, Na Pali's largest valley. The mouth of Kalalau River is 5 miles from Kee Beach along the coast; however, it takes 10 miles of hiking to reach the river by trail owing the many switchbacks in and out of numerous smaller valleys. **Makuaiki Point** in the far distance projects seaward between Nualolo and Milolii Valleys; it is about 9 miles from Kee Beach along the coast. The near-Kee Beach portion of Na Pali is heavily vegetated owing to abundant rainfall (60-70 inches/year). The immediate cliff in this view is only about 800-1000 feet high but steps up to an elevation of over 3500 feet within a mile from the coast. Lava rocks here are of the **5+ million year** old **Na Pali Member** of the **Waimea Canyon Basalt**, the original **shield-building** rocks of Kauai's volcanic mountain-island complex. As late as the 1970s geologists thought that cliffs such as these throughout Hawaii were formed mainly by **wave erosion**, especially from the pounding of North Pacific winter waves. Detailed mapping in the 1980s of the sea floor surrounding the Hawaiian Islands however revealed gigantic submarine landslides, which suggested that the **sea cliffs represented head walls of huge faults that generated the landslides**. There is probably a bit of both.

NA PALI TOPOGRAPHIC PROFILES

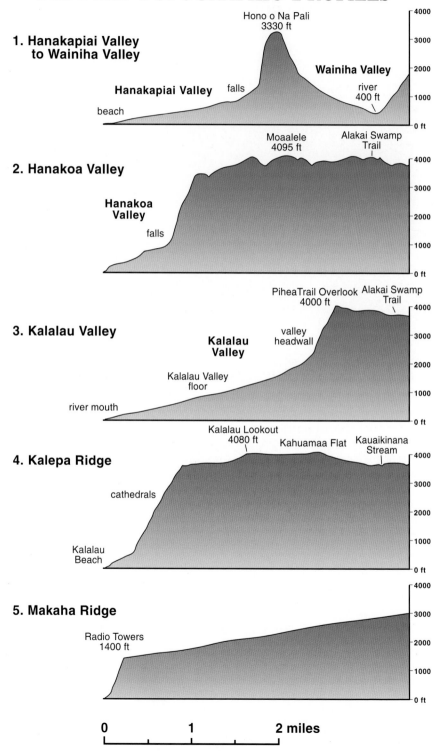

1. Hanakapiai Valley to Wainiha Valley

Hono o Na Pali 3330 ft

Hanakapiai Valley

falls

Wainiha Valley

river 400 ft

beach

2. Hanakoa Valley

Moaalele 4095 ft

Alakai Swamp Trail

Hanakoa Valley

falls

3. Kalalau Valley

Pihea Trail Overlook 4000 ft

Alakai Swamp Trail

Kalalau Valley

valley headwall

Kalalau Valley floor

river mouth

4. Kalepa Ridge

Kalalau Lookout 4080 ft

Kahuamaa Flat

Kauaikinana Stream

cathedrals

Kalalau Beach

5. Makaha Ridge

Radio Towers 1400 ft

0   1   2 miles

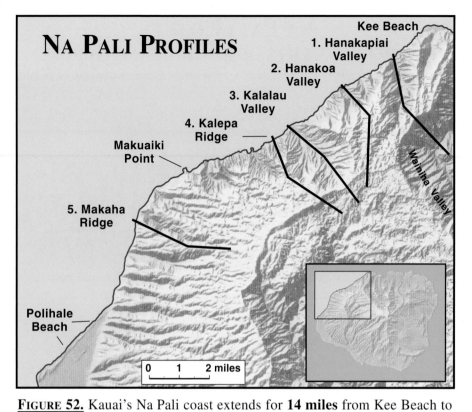

FIGURE 52. Kauai's Na Pali coast extends for **14 miles** from Kee Beach to Polihale Beach. It is dissected by numerous valleys, Kalalau being the largest. The sea cliffs display a wide variety of shapes and heights. The highest vertical cliff faces range up to 1400 feet; however, elevations can reach 4000 feet less than a mile from the coast. The five topographic profiles displayed illustrate a considerable **variation in geomorphic character**. Large valleys such as Kalalau and Hanakapiai have cut the coast back by stream headward erosion; spectacular waterfalls 100s of feet high occur at valley headwalls. Intervening ledges display cliff faces hundreds to thousands of feet high. The plan view (i.e., map) **shape of the pali coastline** also shows significant variation. From Kee Beach to Makuaiki Point, a distance of 8 miles, the shoreline displays a distinct arcuate, **concave seaward shape**, like a big scoop. From Makuaiki Point around to Polihale Beach (6 miles) the **coastline is bowed** in the opposite direction, like a big bulge, and then the curved cliffs extend, with diminishing height, for at least another 12 miles inland to near the mouth of the Waimea River. The Makaha Ridge profile, south of Makuaiki Pt., also displays a considerably different shape than those to the north. All of this suggests that **Na Pali has had a complex origin**. The concave coast may have been created by a **gigantic structural failure** in which much of Kauai's northwest coast slumped (i.e., faulted downward) seaward. The bulge-shaped arcuate coast may have been shaped in part by **wave erosion**. The huge North Pacific winter waves that wrap around and pound Na Pali every year may have some affect over 3-4 million years.

NA PALI COAST
(CATHEDRAL CLIFFS OF KALALAU AND HONOPU)

Kalepa Ridge

Honopu Ridge

Kalalau Beach   Honopu Beach

FIGURE 53. The cliffs behind Kalalau and Honopu Beaches are among Na Pali's most spectacular. At **6 miles** along the coast from Kee Beach these beaches, and associated valleys, are less than half the 14 mile distance of Na Pali from Kee Beach to Polihale Beach. They are most easily accessible via the 11 mile long **Kalalau Trail** or by boat. Here the ridges of Na Pali reach a height of **greater than 3000 feet** less than a mile from the beach. **Geologically** the 5+ million year old **Na Pali Member of the Waimea Canyon Basalt**, which comprises the entire coast, displays only minor variation. The complex of hundreds of weathered and eroded lava flow layers dip seaward, away from the center of the island, at 8-12 degrees and display numerous near-vertical lava dikes. **Sea caves**, resulting from **wave erosion**, are present at the base of sea cliffs along most of the coast. **Annual rainfall** along Na Pali decreases significantly from a high of 60-70 inches at Kee Beach to about 40 inches in the Kalalau Valley area to only about 15-25 inches along Polihale Beach. **Along with the change in rainfall comes change in vegetation and land-forms**. The **cathedral-like cliffs** displayed here, in this sailor's eye view, are extensive only around the Kalalau area. More heavily vegetated, wetter local-ities toward Kee Beach and more arid, less vegetated localities toward Polihale Beach do not display the same sort of fluted leaflike geomorphic features. The precipitous scarp of Na Pali is thought of have formed relatively early in the growth of Kauai's main shield volcanic mountain, some 5 million years ago. The fast-growing volcanic mountain-island became unstable. **Catastrophic structural failures** resulted. Na Pali may originally have been the head wall of a **gigantic slump** like fault. Subsequently the cliffed coast line has had 4-5 million years to become **vegetated**, **weather and erode**. Huge North Pacific **winter waves** also have helped with the sculpting. The

NA PALI COAST
(MAKANA POINT TO POLIHALE)

FIGURE 54. The sea coast portion of Na Pali ends dramatically against the yellowish orange sand of **Polihale Beach** on the semiarid side of Kauai. Sparsely-vegetated lava flow layers of the 5+ million year old **Na Pali Member of the Waimea Canyon Basalt** slope seaward at 8-12 degrees, away from the core of the island. The sea cliff at **Makana Point**, dotted by radio towers and radar tracking facilities, rises precipitously **1400 feet**. The gradual southeastward-climbing slope reaches 3000 feet 3.3 miles from the coast. The prominent **gully-like valleys** displayed along this arid portion of Na Pali undoubtedly were cut by **water erosion** in much wetter times. During the cooler times of global glaciation, sea level would have been as much as 400 feet lower and precipitation/runoff greater, much greater. The original scarp of Na Pali may have been created by catastrophic structural failure (i.e., slump-like down faulting) and wave erosion, but subsequent sculpting was a result of weathering and of erosion by running water, even in this now semidesert setting. **Polihale Beach**, which extends for 3.5 miles from Na Pali to Nohili Point (not shown) is Kauai's, and **Hawaii's largest beach** in terms of sand volume. The sand is composed mainly of fragments of **calcareous algae** and **coral** which have been ripped up by ocean waves, abraded and transported along Na Pali by strong longshore currents to be dumped in **Polihale's beach system**. Most of the sand occurs offshore to depths of 50 feet or more. During the winter when waves are big and coastal turbulence intense, the beach is relatively narrow (down to a few 10s of feet); however, during more gentle summer wave conditions it can grow to 300-500 feet in width. Strong summer trade winds ripping around Na Pali blow finer sand factions obliquely landward to create sparsely-vegetated dunes that reach 100 feet in height. **It's a beach for beach extremists, big, hot, dry, isolated**.

KAUAI'S BEACH SEDIMENTS
THE FINAL GEOLOGIC PRODUCT

The coastal sediments of Hawaii, the **sandy beaches,** are among the most alluring aspects of the islands. Over **47%** of Kauai's perimeter is edged by sand. That's the record for the main high islands at the southeastern end of the archipelago. In terms of sand volume Kauai has the **state's largest beach, Polihale.** It also possesses the **state's longest continuous strand of sandy beach,** the connected Mana Coastal Plain beaches of Polihale, Kekaha and Waimea. Most of Kauai's individual beaches, however, occupy relatively small indentations in the coast line called **"pocket cells".** Such embayments were created by river valleys that were cut during past lower sea levels and then flooded back when sea level rose, all in response to **global glaciation** and **associated sea level fluctuation.** Some beaches are developed behind, and protected by, **fringing reef platforms.** Others occupy tiny indentations along cliffed coasts such as Na Pali. There's a lot of variation from one part of the island's shoreline to another.

To a great extent beach sediment is the **ultimate product** of all the **geological processes** acting on an island. Interpreting the origin of the sedimentary products of a beach, the job of a sedimentologist, is nothing more than interpreting the history of the geological processes that have created the deposit. It's the history of the interaction of the island (i.e., the lithosphere) with the atmosphere, hydrosphere and biosphere. Sediments are the survivors. Their character, i.e., **composition (indicated by color), texture (e.g., grain size) and distribution,** is related to their history of survival in geologically tough environments, from mountain forests and streams to the wave impacted shorelines.

There are **two major types** of sand on Kauai, <u>**volcanic sand**</u> and <u>**calcareous sand**</u> (also commonly called carbonate sand). There are **no naturally occurring quartz sand** beaches in Hawaii. **Volcanic sand** is composed of fragments of **lava rock** and the associated greenish mineral **olivine,** which are eroded from the island and transported by streams and rivers to the shoreline. **Calcareous sand** is made of fragments of biogenic material derived mainly from **fringing reefs.** The main constituents are **coralline algae** (a plant) and skeletons of marine animals such as **coral, foraminifera and mollusks** (clams and snails). They are composed mainly of the **calcium carbonate** ($CaCO_3$) mineral **calcite,** and therefore commonly termed "calcareous" or "carbonate" constituents.

Even though the volcanic island is composed entirely of basaltic lava rock, there is **only one major volcanic sand beach on Kauai, Waimea Beach.** This is due to the fact that the **silica-poor lava rocks** of Hawaii are **very unstable chemically and mineralogically** at the earth's surface. They weather (oxidize and hydrate) and erode extremely fast. Throughout the wetter, and more extensively vegetated portions of Kauai lava rocks breakdown relatively fast from the **chemical interaction of air, water and plants.** Plants produce caustic botanical acids that enhance chemical weathering and they break rocks by rooting. **Soil**, composed of abundant silt and clay size material, is the initial product of such physical and chemical processes. Basically **the island is "rotting".** In most areas, especially along the intensely-weathered windward side of the island, by the time the volcanic rock material reaches the shoreline via some stream it has already been broken down to silt and clay size, so it just stays in suspension in the ocean and floats away from the island. Even beaches developed at river mouths along that side of the island display very low amounts of volcanic sand. In the relatively **dry setting of Waimea Canyon** the **weathering is less chemical and more physical** (abrasive). Much of the disintegrated lava rock is still sand and fine gravel size by the time it reaches the mouth of Waimea River so it is coarse enough to stay on the high-energy, wave-impacted beach. The volcanic sand on Waimea Beach, composed of grayish fragments of lava rock and greenish olivine, ranges from **brownish to greenish gray**. The brownish color is due the presence of iron oxides (a weathering product). **The beach sediment is not black** like some sands of the Island of Hawaii.

    Calcareous skeletal sand is tough. It is derived from the abrasion of the **skeletal material of reefs** and other nearshore areas. The skeletal fragments are transported along and onto the shoreline where they are further abraded, rounded, polished and deposited to form the island's beautiful **yellowish-orange** sandy beaches. Obviously the skeletal fragments are **much more stable, chemically and mineralogically** than are the fragments of Hawaii's volcanic lava rock. The most abundant calcareous sand grain on Kauai's beaches are composed of the abraded remains of a plant, **coralline algae.** Known commonly as "red algae" or "stony algae", coralline algae is a plant that builds its cell walls of the mineral calcite. Most of the **shallow fringing reef platforms** around Kauai display commonly **80-95% cover of coralline algae.** The tough incrusting forms of calcareous algae thrive in such wave dominated high-energy settings. The algae also can survive the short time exposure to air during extreme low tides when the reef platforms are emergent above sea level. Coral, most of which is relatively fragile, can not proliferate in such environmental settings owing to the pounding by Hawaii's big waves and the periodic low tides that **expose the reef platform;** coral dies quickly when out of sea water. Owing to the dominance of coralline algae in such environmental settings, the reefs of Kauai might more correctly be referred to as **"algal reefs"** or at least **"coralgal reefs".**

    The **variability of sand around Kauai** might not be noticeable when casually visiting one beach then another; however, when one places a sample of sand from one beach next to the sand of another beach chances are they will see a difference. Differences are usually in color, which is related directly to grain composition, and grain size, which is related to wave energy at the particular collection site. We have compared sand samples from all the beaches of the island and have noticed essentially that **no two beaches on Kauai are exactly alike.**

The differences in beach sediment is even more dramatic when one compares **sands from the various islands** of Hawaii. On **Hawaii Island** molten lava that flows, and has flowed in the past, directly into the ocean from volcanoes like Kilauea and Mauna Loa chills almost instantly to produce a **jet black volcanic glass.** Fragmentation also takes place during the violent encounter. Subsequent abrasion, rounding and polishing by waves produces the famous, **true black sand beaches** of Hawaii. Near the southern end of Hawaii Island **olive green sand** is produced by the unusual accumulation of olivine grains; they make up 90-95+% of the deposit. At the other end of the archipelago, **bright white sand** is being deposited around the islands of **Midway Atoll.** The atoll is composed mainly of calcareous algae, which bleaches a bright white when fragmented to sand size and exposed to air and sun light. Foraminifera, a sand-size, shelled protozoan, also is abundant in the sands of Midway; it too bleaches to a bright white color.

So, the next time you are on a beautiful Hawaiian beach, think about the sand that is making your visit so enjoyable. The story of the origin of that sand is a story that encompasses the geologic history of the entire island.

BEACHES OF KAUAI

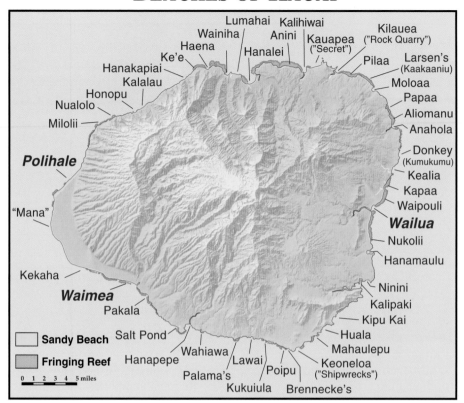

FIGURE 55. The irregularly-shaped **coast line of Kauai** is approximately **111 miles long**. At least **52.5 miles (47%)** is occupied by sandy beaches. [In comparison, Oahu has about 209 miles of shore line with about 65 miles (31%) rimmed by sandy beaches.] A total of **46 Kauai beaches** are indicated above. These are the "main" beaches. At least 40-50 names could be added if the many very small beaches and subdivisions of the larger beaches were included. Names are names; they change much faster than do the beaches themselves. Kauai has the **state's largest beach** (in terms of sand volume), Polihale, and it's **longest continuous strand of sandy beach**, the Mana Coastal Plain beaches of Polihale, to Kekaha and Waimea. Most beaches occupy indentations, or **"pocket cells"** created by river valleys that were cut during lower sea level and then flooded back when sea level rose in response to global glaciation. Some beaches are developed behind, and protected by, **fringing platform reefs**, others occupy tiny indentations along cliffed coasts such at Na Pali. Most beaches are composed of **yellowish-orange sand** derived from the breakdown of the **skeletons of marine reef plants and animals**. Waimea Beach and the much smaller Hanapepe Beach are the only significant beaches composed of **dark greenish gray volcanic sand** derived from the erosion of the island's **basaltic lava rock**.

WAIMEA BEACH
(VOLCANIC SAND)

FIGURE 56. Kauai's Waimea Beach is an **anomaly**. It's the only major **volcanic sand beach** on the island, being composed of **fragments of volcanic (lava) rock** and the greenish mineral **olivine**. As with most anomalies, the volcanic sand along the Waimea shore is a result of **a complex interaction of a number of variables**, in this case mainly **geologic** and **climatic** variables. In general the mineralogically and chemically **unstable**, low silica **lava rock** of Hawaii weathers (oxidizes and hydrates) and erodes extremely fast (geologically speaking). Throughout the wetter, more extensively vegetated portions of Kauai lava rocks breakdown from the **chemical interaction of rocks, air and water. Plants** enhance the chemical degradation of rocks through the production of caustic **botanical acids**, and the break rocks by **rooting**. Soil is the product. In the windward areas of the island by the time the volcanic rock material reaches the shoreline via some stream it is only **silt** and **clay size**, so it just floats away in the ocean. In **Waimea Canyon** there is plenty of running water draining off the Alakai Swamp, but the local climate is much drier and less vegetated. The **weathering is more physical** (abrasive). Disintegrated lava rock is still **sand** and **fine gravel size** by the time it reaches the mouth of the Waimea River so it can **stay at the high-energy shoreline** for a longer time. From this view at the river mouth the volcanic sand is transported, by longshore currents, **2.7 miles** away westward to Oomano Point. Within a half a mile transition zone beyond it merges with Kekaha Beach, which is composed of yellowish-orange, calcareous (i.e., lime) sand derived from as far away as the Na Pali coast and transported eastward and southeastward, also by longshore currents.

POLIHALE BEACH
(WEST SIDE - CALCAREOUS SAND)

FIGURE 57. Polihale Beach, at the extreme western end of the Mana Coastal Plain, is Kauai's, and the state of **Hawaii's, largest** (in terms of sand volume). It is composed mainly of calcareous sand. Calcareous sand is made up of fragments of **coralline algae** (a plant) and skeletons of marine animals such as **coral, foraminifera, clams and snails**. They all are composed mainly of the mineral **calcite**, and therefore commonly referred to as "**calcareous**". **Calcareous skeletal sand is tough**. It is derived from the abrasion of skeletal material in reefs and other nearshore areas. The skeletal fragments are transported along and onto the shoreline where they are further **abraded, rounded, polished and deposited** to form the island's beautiful yellowish-orange sandy beaches. Skeletal fragments are much more stable, chemically and mineralogically, than are fragments of Hawaii's volcanic lava rock. The sand of Polihale was derived mainly from the abrasion of skeletal material probably from as far away as the north shore **reefs in the Anini to Haena area** and transported by **long-shore ocean currents** along the Na Pali coast. The west end of Kauai is sort of a big convergence type dumping ground for such sediment, much of which is stored in shallow off-shore areas (sometimes referred to as a "**beach cells**"). During **summer months**, when waves are relatively small and sand can stay at the shoreline, Polihale Beach can attain widths of **300-500 feet**. However, the huge North Pacific **winter waves** create tremendous turbulence at the shoreline; it is cut back (as shown in photo above) as sand is moved to a more stable location offshore, at least until more gentle summer waves again move it back to the beach. The high **sand dunes** of Polihale are a result of strong landward-directed **trade winds** (most common in summer).

WAILUA BEACH
(EAST SIDE - CALCAREOUS SAND)

Figure 58. The beach at Wailua is just a small portion of an extensive ribbon of **carbonate sand-dominated shoreline** stretching for over **6 miles** north from Nukolii Beach, just north of Hanamaulu Bay, to the north end of Kapaa Beach. Except for the wide bay mouth of the Wailua River the beaches lie behind an **extensive fringing reef platform**. This portion of Kauai also is the most populous, both in terms of residents and visitors; resorts, condominiums and public parks dominate much of the shoreline. And, this is the **windward face of Kauai**. Prevailing **trade winds** (dominate over as much as 80-85% of the year) generate shore directed waves and currents. **Carbonate skeletal material** is derived from **abrasion of the nearshore fringing reef**, and **transported to the shoreline** where it is further **fragmented, rounded, polished and deposited** on the beach. A relatively large volume of **volcanic rock sediment** is discharged into the Wailua Bay area from the Wailua River. That sediment however is mostly **silt** and **clay size**, owing to intense **chemical** and **biochemical** (i.e., plant induced) **weathering** in the drainage basin. The fine **suspended sediment** merely floats offshore away from the shoreline to be deposited on the deep oceanic flanks of Kauai's submerged mountain. Much of the **reddish-brown color** of Wailua River water is from the **botanical acids** generated by plant decay; such acids enhance weathering of the already chemically and mineralogically unstable lava rocks of Kauai. Therefore, **not many dark, lava rock sand grains** can be seen in the beaches of Wailua, and Kapaa.

KAUAI BEACH SEDIMENT COMPOSITION

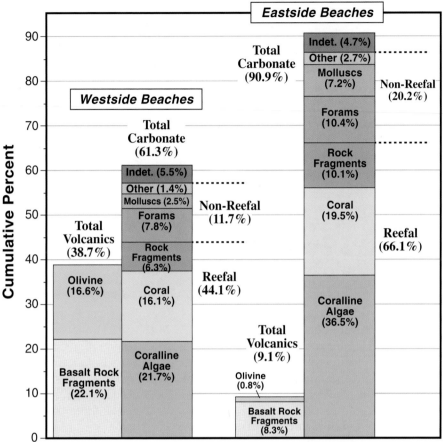

(modified from Blay, Siemers and Siemers, 1997)

FIGURE 59. Sandy beach sediments of Kauai were examined in detail **microscopically** in order to determine sand composition. A total of **130 samples** were analyzed from the **52.5 miles** of the island's beaches. Two main categories were recognized, **volcanic** and **carbonate**. Volcanic grains included fragments of basaltic lava rock and grains of the greenish mineral olivine. In general it was discovered that **volcanic grains are much more abundant on west side beaches** (Hanalei around Na Pali to Waimea and Pakala Beaches) than on east side beaches (Princeville Headlands around the north, east and south shorelines to Salt Pond Beach). West side beaches rim the oldest rocks of the island, Waimea Canyon Basalt; east side beaches rim the younger Koloa Volcanics. Skeletal carbonate sand grains are dominated by **coralline algae**. Coral fragments also are abundant. Foraminifera (single-celled, shelled protozoans) and molluscs (clams and snails) are common, as are fragments of reef rock. The carbonate fraction is indicative of the fact that the **fringing platform reefs of Kauai**, from which much of the beach sediment is derived, are **composed dominantly of coralline algae, not coral**.

84

CORALLINE ALGAE

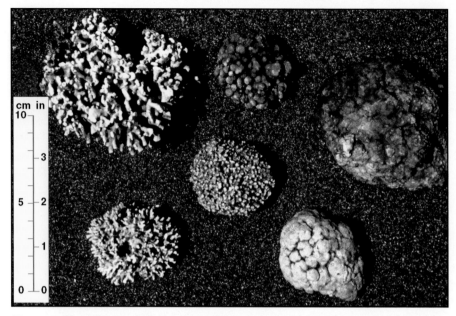

FIGURE 60. Most people are familiar with reef-building coral, or at least they hear the term "coral reef" a lot, especially in Hawaii. However, it turns out that many of **our reefs are dominated by a reef-building <u>plant</u>, coralline algae**. Known commonly also as **"red" algae** or **"stony" algae**, coralline algae is a plant that builds its cell walls of the calcium carbonate ($CaCO_3$) mineral **calcite**. Coral, a colonial animal, also builds it skeleton of carbonate minerals, including calcite and, more commonly, aragonite (both composed of $CaCO_3$). Two main **end-member forms** of coralline algae are common in Hawaii, a **branching form** known as *Porolithon gardineri* and an **encrusting form** known as *Porolithon onkodes*. When alive in the ocean *Porolithon* is **pink** to **purplish red**; out of water it bleaches to a bright white. Good branching form examples of *P. gardineri* are shown by specimens A and B above. At the other end of the spectrum E and F display nodules of the encrusting form, *P. onkodes*. Encrusting red algae is common to extremely abundant over and across the shallow, fringing reef platforms that rim much of Kauai's coastal areas. It encrusts everything, dead corals, shells, fishing weights, sunken boats. Specimens C and D display **intermediate forms** between the encrusting and branching growth forms of *Porolithon*, suggesting that the "species" may only be **ecological growth forms**. **Encrusting forms** are more common in **high energy reef areas**, such as Na Pali which is pounded by huge waves every winter. **Branching forms** are more abundant in relatively **low energy backreef areas** protected from the brunt of wave impact. Most **shallow fringing reef platforms** around Kauai display commonly **80-95% cover of coralline algae**. The reefs might more correctly be referred to as **"algal reefs"**, or at least **"coralgal reefs"**. It's no wonder that coralline algae is the dominant sand grain type in the island's beach sediments.

SELECTED BEACH SAND OF KAUAI

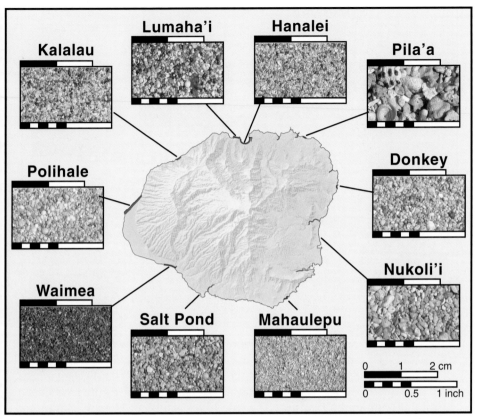

FIGURE 61. Like most other aspects of Kauai's coastal area, beach sediments display considerable variation. These close-up photos of selected sand samples are reproduced at true scale, **no magnification**. They display obvious variation in color, which is directly related to **composition**, and **grain size**. Kauai's beaches most commonly are a **yellowish-orange color**, Polihale, Mahaulepu, Nukolii being good examples. They are composed mainly of coralline algae and carbonate skeletal material, including coral, foraminifera, molluscs (clams and snails). Some beaches are much coarser grained in general, like Pilaa. Others commonly are much finer grained, like Mahaulepu. **Grain size** can be related to **seasonal changes in wave energy** or to **location**, such as open high-energy beach faces verses relatively low-energy backreef areas. The **dark greenish gray** sand of Waimea Beach is initiative of its **volcanic sand content**, including fragments of lava rock and the greenish mineral olivine. Lumahai and Kalalau beach sediments are composed mainly of carbonate skeletal grains, but also contain abundant olivine. Lumahai Beach sediment commonly contains 30-50% olivine, giving it a greenish tint. With so many variables involved one should expect such variation.

Hawaiian Beach Sediment

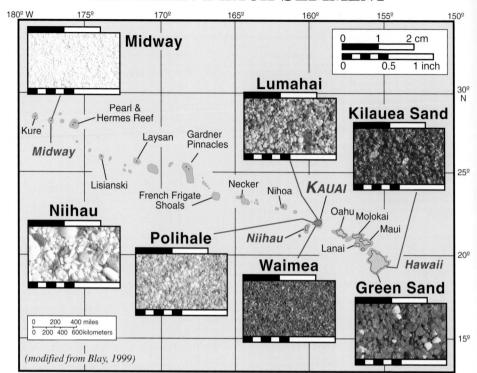

FIGURE 62. The sands of Hawaii possess considerable variation in composition, which is indicated megascopically by color. The close-up photos shown here of sand selected from the islands of Hawaii, Kauai and Midway are reproduced at true scale, **no magnification**. The true **black sands of Hawaii Island** are produced by the violent chilling and fragmentation of 2000+ degree molten lava as it flows directly into the ocean. Most of Hawaii's black sand is associated with Kilauea Volcano in the Puna District of the Big Island. The quickly-chilled lava produces **amorphous** (i.e., noncrystalline) **black glass**. The relatively soft fragments are easily rounded and polished in the high-energy wave-dominated windward Puna coastal setting. The famous **Green Sand (Papakolea) Beach** at Makana Bay near South Point is composed mainly of sand-size grains of the mineral **olivine**. The green grains are concentrated in an indented shoreline setting where an olivine-rich cinder cone is being slowly eroded by waves. The **whitest sand** we have observed for the State of Hawaii is that from **Midway Atoll**. Sand is composed mainly of bleached and abraded fragments of **coralline algae**, minor to only moderate amounts of **coral**, and sand-size grains of **foraminifera**, a shelled protozoan. Some Niihau beach sediment is very light colored. The sands of Kauai show considerable variation in composition, and therefore color. The **volcanic sand of Waimea Beach** is actually a **dark greenish gray** color, not black, being composed of **weathered lava rock fragments** and **olivine**. Yellowish-orange **calcareous sand**, such as that displayed for Polihale, is common on Kauai. With its calcareous-olivine mix the sand of Lumahai Beach it takes on a greenish tint.

CONCLUDING REMARKS

Most people, even those with training in geology, have difficulty dealing with the concept of geologic time. Graphic scenarios never seem to adequately display the vastness of time recorded by the Earth. The Kauai/Earth time line (following page) lists a few events of interest in an attempt to integrate geologic and human history within the 10 orders of magnitude of geologic time.

The geologic and natural history of the present island of Kauai (age greater than 5.1 million years) represents only 0.11% of the time since the origin of the Earth about 4.6 billion years ago. Human history extends to 4-5 million years ago (about the time of the first hominids). The archaeological, anthropological and Hawaiian cultural histories on Kauai occupy only the last 2,000 years, or only about 0.04% of the age of the island. Polynesian and Hawaiian oral history on the island extends to the time of the first occupants. Their written history encompasses less than 230 years, since the time of the first significant contact by Europeans.

The early inhabitants of the isolated volcanic islands of Hawaii were limited in terms of available natural earth materials. Although displaying an advanced culture in terms of language, social structure, craftsmanship and navigational skills, they possessed only stone-age implements at the time of European contact. Hawaiian volcanic rocks do not yield basic metals such as copper, tin and iron, which were so important to the developing cultures of Asia and Europe. Polynesian implements were made of varieties of volcanic rock, limestone (reefrock and beachrock), various woods and plants, bones (including those of humans), shells and the like. Pottery was not produced owing in part to the poor clays generated from the weathering of volcanic rock. Mortar and other types of cement were not used since the Polynesians did not possess that technology, even though limestone is rather plentiful around many of the islands. Obviously this is a good example of how the physical setting affects human cultural development, especially as seen through the eyes of an archaeologist/anthropologist.

Finally, it is interesting to note the changes in the interpretation of the geologic history of the Hawaiian Islands over the last few decades. It might surprise you to know that it was not until the early 1960's, that the geological theories of plate tectonics and magmatic hot spots originated and that the first radiometric dates of the island's volcanic rocks were published. Before that most geologists thought that the Hawaiian Islands had been produced by volcanic eruptions along a long fissure in the oceanic crust. Relative ages of the high volcanic islands, generally with Kauai being the oldest and Hawaii being the youngest, were based on degrees of erosion and the biogeographic distribution of native plants and

KAUAI / EARTH TIME LINE
YEARS BEFORE PRESENT

4,600,000,000	-- origin of the Earth
2,500,000,000	-- blue-green algae appear
570,000,000	-- beginning of Paleozoic (invertebrates)
Northern end Emperor -- Seamounts — 70,000,000	
Hawaiian / Emperor chain -- dogleg bend — 43,000,000	
Midway islands, Hawaii -- 28,000,000	
Oldest volcanic rocks -- island of *KAUAI* — 5,100,000	
4,500,000	-- early Hominids
2,400,000	-- earliest human stone technology
600,000	-- "Old Stone Age" (Lower Paleolithic)
youngest volcanic rocks -- island of *KAUAI* — 520,000	
Kohala volcanic rocks -- island of Hawaii — 430,000	
250,000	-- *Homo neanderthalensis*
100,000	-- *Homo sapiens*
30,000	-- Cro-Magnon man replaces Neanderthals
Sea level in Hawaii -- -360 to -390 feet — 21,000	
10,000	-- end of "New Stone Age" (Neolithic)
9,000	-- Copper Age
6,000	-- Bronze Age
3,000	-- Iron Age
Sea level in Hawaii +5 to +6 feet — 2,000	-- Polynesian discovery of Hawaii
500	-- European discovery / exploration of Pacific Ocean
220	-- British contact with Hawaii
Hawaii K-Ar dates; Plate Tectonics; Hot Spot Theory -- 40	
10	-- Hurricane Iniki on *KAUAI*

FIGURE 63. See text for discussion.

animals. It is only somewhat recent thought which indicates that Hawaii's volcanic mountain/islands were formed successively as the 3-5 mile thick oceanic crust of the Pacific Tectonic Plate moved northwestward (at a rate of about 3.4 inch/yr) across the Hawaiian Magmatic Hot Spot.

So what can be expected for Kauai? Nihoa is the next Hawaiian island to the northwest. It is an uninhabitable rock less than a mile long and less than 900 ft high, compared with the Garden Island of Kauai which is 32 miles long and over 5,200 ft high. Nihoa's volcanic rocks have been dated at 7.2 million years, compared with Kauai at 5.1 million years. Assuming that Nihoa was at least 5,000 ft high 2.1 million years ago, Kauai would have to subside and be eroded at a rate of 2,050 ft/million years (or at about 1 inch every 40 years) to reach that level. Nihoa is 162 miles northwest of Kauai. With the Pacific Tectonic Plate moving at 3.4 inch/yr it would take about 3 million years for Kauai to move to Nihoa's present location. Using such scenarios, one can estimate that it will take something around 2 to 3 million years for Kauai to be transformed from one of the Earth's most beautiful islands to one preferred mainly by sea birds.

GLOSSARY

Absolute Age. The geologic age of rocks and related geologic features or events given in units of time, usually years, rather than in relation to other geologic features (i.e., "younger" or "older" than). In Hawaii the absolute age of volcanic rocks is determined by radiometric dating (see radiometric dates).

Ahupuaa. Ancient Hawaiian land division, commonly extending from it's apex in the central part of an island to the shore and reef.

Alkalic Lava/Basalt. A fine-grained (crystalline) dark-colored volcanic rock poor in silica and relatively rich in minerals with elements such as sodium and potassium. In Hawaii post-shield and rejuvenation stage lavas are mainly alkalic basalt with plagioclase feldspar, calcium-rich augite and olivine.

Aragonite. A calcium carbonate ($CaCO_3$) mineral with orthorhombic crystal structure. It has a greater density and hardness, and less distinct cleavage than calcite (also composed of $CaCO_3$) and is less stable than calcite at Earth's surface temperature and pressure. Organisms such as corals and molluscs (both pelecypods and gastropods) commonly produce skeletal material composed of aragonite, which eventually converts to calcite.

Atoll. In general, a ring-shaped coral/algal reef appearing as a low, roughly circular to elliptical island with a central lagoon and surrounding open ocean. Such low, reef islands are common in the central and western Pacific Ocean. Northwest of Kauai atolls have formed as high volcanic islands have subsided and been replaced by the fringing reefs that continued their upward growth.

Basalt. A fine-grained (crystalline) dark- to medium-colored (i.e., gray to black) igneous rock formed when molten lava is extruded onto the Earth's surface and cools rapidly. When erupted from volcanoes, basaltic lava tends to be fluid and floods evenly over large areas. Basalt covers about 70% of the Earth's surface as it is the main rock type forming the ocean floor. The Hawaiian Islands consist primarily of basalt.

Bathymetry. The measurement of water depths in the ocean and charting of the topography of the ocean floor.

Calcareous. Containing calcite, such as "calcareous sand" which is made up fragments of the skeleton of organisms composed of calcite.

Calcite. A rock-forming mineral composed of calcium carbonate ($CaCO_3$), with trigonal crystal structure and perfect rhombohedral cleavage. Calcite is more stable at Earth's surface than aragonite (also composed of $CaCO_3$). Most coralline algae, which is a principle constituent of coral/algal reefs, and organisms like foraminifers and echinoderms produce skeletal material composed of calcite. Uplifted reef platforms and beachrock commonly are cemented by calcite.

Caldera. A large (1 to >10 km) roughly circular volcanic crater formed by the collapse of the central portion of a volcano as the magma chamber below empties. Calderas are characterized by steep sides and a flat bottom like those of Kilauea Crater on the island of Hawaii.

Carbonate. Composed of minerals containing the anionic structure CO_3, such as calcite or aragonite which have the composition $CaCO_3$.

Clay/Claystone. Clay is both a textural (e.g., grain-size) term and a compositional term. Clay particles are less than 4 microns (0.004 mm) in diameter; a claystone is a rock composed mainly of clay-size particles. A group of minerals known as "clay minerals" includes minerals like kaolinite, illite, and montmorillonite, which also commonly are clay size. Soils contain abundant clay-size particles and clay minerals.

Conglomerate. A coarse-grained sedimentary rock composed of rounded, gravel-size grains (i.e., pebbles, cobbles and boulders; diameter >2 mm) which have been cemented, and/or pressed together to form a rock. In Hawaii such sedimentary deposits are common in mountain streams and along high-energy coasts.

Coral. General name for group of bottom-dwelling, sessile, marine invertebrate organisms that belong to the class Anthozoa (phylum Coelenterata); common as reef-building organisms in warm tropical marine waters.

Coral/Algal Reef. A ridge- or mound-like organic structure built mainly by corals and coralline algae. In Hawaii, Tertiary to Holocene, and modern, reefs are generally referred to as "coral" reefs but may actually be composed mainly of coralline algae, which encrusts and binds the structure.

Coralline Algae. A type of algae (a plant) that builds its cells of calcite; also commonly called "red" algae or "stony" algae.

Cross-Bedded. Layering in sediments and sedimentary rocks that is inclined with respect to a horizontal plane; common in beach and sand dune deposits.

Debris Avalanche/Flow. A rapid (avalanche) or slow (flow) mass movement of material (commonly water-saturated) downslope in response to gravity. In Hawaii such destructive events occur both above (i.e., subaerial) and below (i.e., subaqueous) sea level owing to the destruction of the islands by the atmosphere and hydrosphere.

Dike. A cross-cutting (discordant) tabular (or planar) rock feature, usually an igneous intrusive, which cuts at relatively high angles across surrounding planar rocks (e.g., older lava flows).

Effusive Eruption. Volcanic eruption in which liquid molten lava is the principal product.

Endemic. Referring to organisms (plants and animals) only found in one location, commonly the location in which they evolved.

Explosive Eruption. Volcanic eruption in which molten magma is forcefully ejected, such as cinder and volcanic bombs that are thrown high in the air above a volcanic vent.

Fault. A fracture or break in a series of rocks along which movement has taken place. The movement may vary from a few centimeters to a few kilometers.

Fracture. A general term for any break in a rock, whether or not it shows displacement, owing to mechanical failure. Fractures include cracks, joints and faults.

Foraminifera. Any protozoan (i.e., single-celled organism) belonging to the order Foraminiferida, characterized by the presence of a skeleton composed commonly of calcite. Foraminifers are common constituents of Hawaii's sandy beaches.

Fringing Reef. Biogenic structure, commonly built of coral and coralline algae, that forms from the shoreline and grows seaward to produce a platform. Such reefs are common in Hawaii owing to the steep nature of the nearshore slope.

Geologic Formation. Group of rocks that have been described, delineated and named in order to be distinguished from other rock groups; may be subdivided into a number of less voluminous or extensive members.

Geologic Member. Group of rocks that have been described, delineated and named and are part of, and therefore less extensive than, a formation.

GLORIA. Acronym for "Geologic Long-Range Inclined Asdic", a side-looking sonar system for recording acoustic back-scattered energy from the sea-floor. Such a system recently has been used successively to examine the deep seafloor around the Hawaiian Islands.

Graben. A structural feature where an elongate block of the earth's crust, bordered by normal faults, has been down-dropped, or lowered, relative to the surrounding rocks.

High Island. In the Pacific Ocean a volcanic mountain/island for which the island portion still extends well above sea level (usually at least several hundred feet). The eight main Hawaiian Islands of Hawaii, Maui, Molokai, Lanai, Kahoolawe, Oahu, Kauai and Niihau are excellent examples of high islands.

Holocene. An epoch of the Quaternary period from the end of the Pleistocene to the present time; commonly referring to the last 10,000 years or.

Hot Spot (Magmatic). A stationary cylindrical/cone-shaped magma chamber within the upper mantle of the Earth that intermittently pushes magma upward through the crust as the plate moves across the chamber. The Hawaiian Island Magmatic Hot Spot is probably the Earth's best example of such a feature.

Hydration. Chemical reaction in which water, commonly in the form of OH- (the hydroxyl ion), is added to a mineral.

Hyaloclastic. Sediment produced by the reaction (usually violently explosive) of molten lava entering water, which causes chilling and fragmentation.

Isohyetal Lines. Contour lines on a map connecting points of equal rainfall.

Lava. A molten extrusive material (magma) and the rock formed from its cooling and solidification.

Lava Flow. A lateral, surface outpouring of molten lava from a vent or fissure; also the solidified body of rock that is so formed.

Leeward. The side of a hill, slope, or island that faces away and is sheltered from the wind.

Limestone. A sedimentary rock consisting chiefly of calcium carbonate, primarily in the form of the mineral calcite. Geologically young limestones around the Hawaiian Islands (e.g., coral/algal reefs, beachrock) may also contain significant amounts of the calcium carbonate mineral aragonite.

Lithify. To change to stone, especially to consolidate from a loose sediment to a sedimentary rock.

Low Island. In the Pacific Ocean a relatively low relief coral/algal reef atoll, bank, shoal, etc. composed of calcium carbonate ($CaCO_3$) organic deposits. In contrast to volcanic high islands, they usually extend only a few feet, or tens of feet above sea level. Many of the Hawaiian Islands between Kauai and Midway Island are low islands.

Magma. Naturally occurring molten, mobile rock material generated at high temperature and pressure in the lower crust and upper mantle of the Earth. Such material is capable of intrusion into the crust or extrusion onto the Earth's surface (both below and above sea level). Below Hawaii magma is formed by the melting of upper mantle crystalline rocks at 60-170 km (35-105 mi) depth.

Mass Wasting. A general term for the loosening and downslope, gravity-driven movement of soil and rock; e.g., water-saturated landslides, debris avalanches. The Hawaiian volcanic islands have undergone extensive destruction by both subaerial (above sea level) and submarine mass wasting of their slopes in response to interaction with the atmosphere and hydrosphere.

Mollusc. A solitary invertebrate belonging to the phylum Mollusca; including pelecypods (clams) and gastropods (snails).

Mud/Mudstone. Fine-grained sedimentary material/or rock, of any composition, with grain size of less than 62 microns (0.062 mm); includes silt and clay size material. Soils are composed mainly of mud-size material.

Oceanic Mountain/Island. Mountain (usually volcanic) within the ocean basin, the top of which extends above sea level. The eight main islands of Hawaii are excellent examples of ocean volcanic mountain/islands.

Oceanic Ridge. A mid-ocean mountain range extending across the ocean floor; usually a broad fractured swell with a central rift valley and rugged topography; the location of the source of new crustal material where the sea floor is spreading.

Olivine. A green mineral composed of $(Mg,Fe)_2SiO_4$, which is common in basic rocks such as basalt. Olivine crystals are common in some of the basaltic lavas of the Hawaiian Islands; they commonly weather out and are concentrated in some beach sands, which then take on a greenish appearance.

Orographic Effect. Rainfall that results when moisture-laden air is forced upward over a high barrier into a cooler altitude causing the moist air to condense into rain droplets. Such is the case in the Hawaiian Islands where moist, tradewind-driven air is forced up and over the high volcanic mountain/islands.

Oxidation. Chemical reaction occurring during weathering in which oxygen (O_2), is added to a mineral.

Paleowind. Ancient wind direction determined by the measurement of cross-bedding in sand dunes.

Pali. Hawaiian word for Cliff.

Pillow Lava/Basalt. A general term used for lavas displaying pillow-shaped masses. Such shapes result from the rapid cooling of molten lavas when they encounter water; they range in size from a few inches to a few feet in diameter. Pillow lavas are common in Hawaii where mountain/islands were formed by extrusion of lava directly on to the sea floor and by lava flowing down the island and into the ocean.

Plate Tectonics. Geologic theory for the origin of the Earth's surface in which extensive, curved, plate-shaped portions of the oceanic and continental crust are moving in relation to each other.

Pleistocene. An epoch of the Quaternary Period which extends for approximately 1 million years, except for the Holocene of the last 10,000 years.

Post-Shield Stage. The stage in volcano building that occurs after the main shield-building stage and commonly includes partial collapse/subsidence (e.g., caldera formation) and minor eruptions that partially fill such collapse structures.

Radiometric Dating. A method of calculating an absolute age (in years) for geologic materials by measuring the presence of radioactive elements and their decay products; e.g., potassium-40/argon-40. Such elements have known decay rates so the relative amounts of original material and decay products is related to the amount of time the material has been decaying. In Hawaii the absolute ages of volcanic materials have been determined by radiometric dating.

Rejuvenation Stage. Relatively late stage of development in the life of an oceanic mountain/island volcano in which lavas and ash are extruded through fissures and vents. The last stage of extrusion commonly involves explosive eruptions that form cinder cones. On Kauai the rejuvenation stage of volcano building continued until about 500,000 years ago and included both lava flows and explosive eruptions from as may as 40 volcanic vents.

Relative Age. The geologic age of a rock, or geologic feature/event only in relation to other rocks, features or events. Therefore, the ages of rocks and geologic features or events can be referred to only as "older" or "younger", and not in terms of absolute time, such as years.

Rift Zone. In Hawaii a zone of fractures and volcanic eruption that extends away from the area of the summit crater.

Sand/Sandstone. Sedimentary material/rock composed of grains (of any mineral or chemical composition) with diameter between silt (62 microns; 0.062 mm) and granule (2000 microns; 2 mm). Most beaches, and associated wind-blown dune deposits in Hawaii are composed of sand size sediment.

Scarp. A line of cliffs produced by faulting or erosion; an abbreviated form of escarpment.

Seamount. Volcanic mountain/island whose top is below the surface of the ocean owing to subsidence (i.e., sinking) and/or erosion. All of the previous volcanic mountain/islands of the Emperor Volcanic Chain and some of the volcanic mountain/islands of the Hawaiian Volcanic Chain have been eroded and sunk below sea level to form seamounts.

Shield-Building Stage. Initial stage of volcanic mountain/island in which the main body of the mountain is built by volcanic eruptions both below and above sea level. The rounded profile of Hawaiian volcanic mountain/islands displays the shape of a shield such as that used by Roman warriors.

Shield Volcano. A volcano in the shape of a flattened dome, broad and low, built by flows of very fluid, basaltic lava.

Sill. A tabular (or planar) rock feature, usually an igneous intrusive, that parallels (or is concordant with) the planar structure of the surrounding rock (e.g., older lava flow layers).

Subaerial. Occurring beneath the atmosphere or in the open air; especially said of conditions and processes (such as erosion) that exist or operate above sea level.

Subduction Zone. An elongate region along which a crustal block descends relative to another crustal block; commonly at the boundary of colliding oceanic and continental tectonic plates.

Subsidence. The sinking, or settling. of a large portion of the Earth's crust relative to its surrounding parts. All of the volcanic mountain/islands of the Hawaiian Islands have undergone various amounts of subsidence, some greater than 10,000 feet.

Tectonic Plate. Large portion of Earth's crust (i.e., oceanic or/and continental) which moves in response to lateral forces in the upper mantle. The extensive chain of volcanic mountain/islands, atolls, seamounts, etc. of the Hawaiian-Emperor Volcanic Chain formed as the Pacific Tectonic Plate moved northward and northwestward across the Hawaiian Magmatic Hot Spot in the Earth's mantle.

Tholeiitic Lava/Basalt. Finely-crystalline volcanic rock composed primarily of plagioclase, pyroxene (augite) and iron oxide minerals; with little or no olivine. Such volcanic rocks comprise most of the Hawaiian volcanic mountain/island masses.

Topographic Profile. Cross-section displaying the changing shape of a land surface.

Topography. The general configuration of a land surface including its relief and the position of its natural and man-made features.

Tsunami. A gravitational sea wave produced by any large-scale, short-duration disturbance of the ocean floor, such as a submarine landslide.

Volcanic Chain. A linear cluster of volcanic mountain/islands; e.g., Hawaiian-Emperor Volcanic Chain.

Volcanic Sand. Sand produced by explosive eruption of a volcano or by the erosion, transport and resedimentation of volcanic rock material of sand size.

Watershed. The region, such as a drainage basin and valley catchment, that is drained by a stream and its tributaries.

Windward. The side of a topographic feature, such as an island, that faces the direction from which the wind is blowing.

REFERENCES

BLAY, C.T., 1999, Compositional analysis of Hawaiian beach sediments: an indicator of source, process and coastal change; *in* Fletcher, C.H. and Matthews, J.V., eds., The Non-Steady State of the Inner Shelf and Shoreline: Coastal Change on the Time Scale of Decades to Millenia in the Late Quaternary: Inaugural Mtg IGCP Project 437, Univ. Hawaii, Nov. 9-12, abstracts with program, p. 55-58.

BLAY, C.T. and LONGMAN, M.W., 2001, Stratigraphy and sedimentology of Pleistocene and Holocene carbonate eolianites, Kauai, Hawaii, USA; *in* Abegg, F.E., Loope, D.B. and Harris, P.M., eds., Modern and Ancient Carbonate Eolianites: Sedimentology, Sequence Stratigraphy and Diagenesis: SEPM Special Pub. 71, Soc. Sedimentary Geology, Tulsa, p. 93-115.

BLAY, C.T., SIEMERS, R.J. and SIEMERS, T.J., 1997, Character and origin of beach sediments, island of Kauai, Hawaii: Geol. Soc. Amer., Cordilleran Sec., abstracts with program, v. 29, p. 5.

BURNEY, D.A., JAMES, H.F., BURNEY, L.P., OLSON, S.L., KIKUCHI, W., WAGNER, W.L., BURNEY, M., McCLOSKY, D., KIKUCHI, D., GRADY, F.V., GAGE, R., and NISHEK, R., 2001, Fossil evidence for a diverse biota from Kauai and its transformation since human arrival: Ecol. Mono., v. 71, no. 4, p. 615-641.

BURNEY, L.P. AND BURNEY, D.A., 2003, Charcoal stratigraphies for Kauai and the timing of human arrival: Pacific Science, v. 57, no. 2, p. 211-226.

CARSON, H.L., and CLAGUE, D.A., 1995, Geology and Biogeography of the Hawaiian Islands. In Wagner, W. L., and Funk, V. A., eds., Hawaiian Biogeography; Evolution on a Hot Spot: Smithsonian Institution Press, Wash., DC, p. 14-29.

CLAGUE, D.A., and BOHRSON, W., 1987, Geologic field guide to Waimea Canyon, Kauai, Hawaii: Geol. Soc. Amer., Cent. Fld Guide - Cord. Sec., p. 1-4.

CLAGUE, D.A., and DALRYMPLE, G.B., 1987, The Hawaiian-Emperor volcanic chain. In Decker, R.W., Wright, T. L., and Stauffer, P.H., eds., Volcanism in Hawaii: U.S. Geol. Survey Prof. Paper 1350, U.S. Gov. Printing Off., Wash., DC, p. 1-54.

CLAGUE, D.A., and DALRYMPLE, G.B., 1988, Age and petrology of alkalic postshield and rejuvenated-shield lava from Kauai, Hawaii: Contrib. Mineral Petrol, v. 99, p. 202-218.

CLAGUE, D.A., and DALRYMPLE, G.B., 1989, Tectonics, geochronology and origin of the Hawaiian-Emperor volcanic chain. In Winterer, E.L., Hussong, D.M., and Decker, R.W., eds., The Geology of North America; Volume N, The Eastern Pacific Ocean and Hawaii: The Geol. Soc. America, Boulder, CO, p. 188-217.

DANA, J.D., 1849, United States Exploring Expedition, under the command of Charles Wilkes, 1832-1842: v. 10, p. 262-279.

DAY, A.G., ed., 1966, Mark Twain's Letters from Hawaii: Univ. Hawaii Press, Honolulu, 298 p.

GRAVES, W., et al., 1985, Earth's Dynamic Crust: National Geographic Soc., Wash. DC, 1 sheet.

HAZLETT, R.W., and HYNDMAN, D.W., 1996, Roadside Geology of Hawaii: Mountain Press Pub. Co., Missoula, 307 p.

HINDS, N.E.A., 1930, The geology of Kauai and Hiihau: B.P. Bishop Mus., Bull. 71, 103 p.

KLEIN, F.W., and KOYANAGI, R.Y., 1988, The seismicity and tectonics of Hawaii. *in* Winter, E.L., Hussong, D.M. and Decker, R.W., eds., The Geology of North

America; Volume N, The Eastern Pacific Ocean and Hawaii: The Geological Society of America, Boulder, CO, p. 238-252.

MANOA MAPWORKS, 1983, State of Hawaii: map at scale of 1:439,500, The Bess Press, Inc., Honolulu, 1 sheet,

McDOUGALL, I., 1979, Age of shield-building volcanism of Kauai and linear migration of volcanism in the Hawaiian Island chain: Earth and Planetary Science Letters, v. 46, p. 31-42.

MACDONALD, G.A., ABBOTT, A.T., and PETERSON, F.L., 1983, Volcanoes in the Sea: The Geology of Hawaii, 2nd edition: Univ. Hawaii Press, Honolulu, 517 p.

MACDONALD, G.A., DAVIS, D.A., and COX, D.C., 1960, Geology and ground-water resources of the island of Kauai, Hawaii: Hawaii Division of Hydrography, Bull. 13, 212 p, colored geologic map.

MOORE, J.G., and CLAGUE, D.A., 1992, Volcano growth and evolution of the island of Hawaii: Bulletin of Geological Society of America, v. 104, p. 1471-1484.

MOORE, J.G., CLAGUE, D.A., HOLCOMB, R.T., LIPMAN, P.W., NORMARK, W.E., and TORRESAN, M.E., 1989, Prodigious submarine landslides on the Hawaiian Ridge: Journal of Geophysical Research, v. 94, p. 17,465-17,484

MOORE, J.G., NORMARK, W.R., and HOLCOMB, R.T., 1994, Giant Hawaiian underwater landslides: Science, v. 264, p. 46-47.

MOORE, J.G., NORMARK, W.R., and HOLCOMB, R.T., 1994, Giant Hawaiian Landslides: Annual Review Earth and Planetary Sciences, v. 22, p. 119-144.

PERNETTA, J., 1994, Atlas of the Oceans: Rand McNally, Reed Int'l Books, Ltd., 208 p.

PETERSON, D.W., and MOORE, R.B., 1987, Volcanism in Hawaii. Geologic history and evolution of geologic concepts, island of Hawaii: U.S. Geological Survey Prof. Paper 1350, p. 149-189.

POWERS, S., 1917, Tectonic lines in the Hawaiian Islands: Geol. Soc. America Bull., v. 28, p. 501-514.

ROELOFS, F., 1993, Canyon Country Excursions: Waimea Canyon and Kaluapuhi Trail: Moanalua Gardens Foundation, Honolulu, 32 p.

SCHROEDER, T., 1993, Chapter 2, Climate Controls; in Sanderson, M., ed., Prevailing Trade Winds: Weather and Climate in Hawaii: Univ. Hawaii Press, Honolulu, p. 12-36.

SHARP, W.D., and CLAGUE, D.A., 2002, An older, slower Hawaii-Emperor bend: Eos, Trans. Am. Geophys. Union, v. 83, no. 47, p. F1282.

STEARNS, H.T., 1946, Geology and groundwater resources of the island of Hawaii: Hawaii Division of Hydrography, Bull. 9, 363 p., colored geologic map.

TAKAHASHI, E., et al., 2002, Hawaiian Volcanoes; Deep Underwater Perspectives: Am. Geophysical Union, Geophys. Monograph 128, 418 p.

TARDUNO, J.A., et al., 2003, The Emperor Seamounts: Southward motion of the Hawaiian hotspot plume in Earth's mantle: Science, v. 301, p. 1064-1069.

WALKER, D.A., 1994, Tsunamis in Hawaii: Tsunami Memorial Inst., Haleiwa, HI, 1 sheet.

WALKER, ., 1990, Geology and volcanology of the Hawaiian Islands: Pacific Science, v. 44, p. 315-347.